Dancing in the Moonlight
Embracing the Sacred in the Dying Time

A Guide for Caregivers and Anyone Facing the End-of-Life

Karin Nemri

Dancing in the Moonlight
Embracing the Sacred in the Dying Time
All Rights Reserved.
Copyright © 2020 Karin Nemri
v3.0

The opinions expressed in this manuscript are solely the opinions of the author and do not represent the opinions or thoughts of the publisher. The author has represented and warranted full ownership and/or legal right to publish all the materials in this book.

This book may not be reproduced, transmitted, or stored in whole or in part by any means, including graphic, electronic, or mechanical without the express written consent of the publisher except in the case of brief quotations embodied in critical articles and reviews.

Echo Rising Publications

ISBN: 978-0-578-22449-7

Cover Photo © 2020 Karin Nemri. All rights reserved - used with permission.

PRINTED IN THE UNITED STATES OF AMERICA

Praise for
Dancing in the Moonlight
Embracing the Sacred in the Dying Time

Dancing in the Moonlight is not only a touching and tender memoir about how the author and her family dealt with the terminal illness of her father, but a book that illustrates and illuminates the profound mysteries that occur as death approaches. It is full of spiritual and practical wisdom, too, and anyone who has to deal with the death of a loved one will be grateful to Karin Nemri for the gift of her beautiful and moving story.

-- Kenneth Ring, Ph.D., author of
Lessons from the Light and *Waiting to Die.*

Karin Nemri has written a short but absorbing autobiographical book that I read in one session. Karin, a gifted Aiijii healer, interweaves the dying process through the process of life. The book metaphorically reflects a day: Dawn, Midday, Twilight and Midnight. By the end of the story, each part of the journey comes full circle. 'Dancing in the Moonlight' is as much a guide as a story about a family, particularly Karin and her relationship with her father and also her mother. This book reflects a series of revelations about one of the most feared mysteries of our physical existence—our death. It is about possible soul relationships and even the impacts of the near-death experience on development.

-- Dr. Vernon Neppe

I always thought that someone should write a story or a book about what people who have had a near death experience end up doing with the rest of their lives. This book is the story of one such person and how she was able to integrate her remembrance of her experience into the care of her father when he was terminally ill. Her extensive knowledge of the caregiving aspects of hospice care and how to deal with the multiple losses and emotions that naturally come with this feared time of life will be the perfect escort to help you on your own journey.

I'm so proud of Karin for writing this book and sharing her commitment to helping people understand what the dying time may have to offer. So if my words move you in any way, read this book and be prepared to dance!

-- Dannion Brinkley, International New York Times best-selling Author of *Saved by the Light*

I dedicate this book to my sister Donna, my brother Bob, my Aunt Ann and my three children, Rashid, Saida and Hassan. We are family. I love you.

Acknowledgements

I would like to express gratitude and love to my friends who believed in my project since its inception a decade ago and for your continued encouragement, your patience, and your honest opinions and suggestions. I would not have been able to get over the hurdles without you. You will always be my heroes.

Boyce, Bailey, Evelyn, Tina, Michael

TABLE OF CONTENTS

Dawn
1

Midday
55

Twilight
127

Midnight
153

Conclusion
177

Afterward
179

About the Author
193

DAWN

Chapter One

> *"One finds one's story, one's calling, one's true vocation in the midst of one's broken body, one's broken dreams, one's shattered self."*
> ~ Janice Brewi and A. Brennan

IT WAS THE summer of 2005 when my father and I first began to engage in conversations about death and the afterlife. It was also when he first learned that he may have pancreatic cancer. Actually, it was me who did all the talking. I brought up my near-death experience that had taken place when I was fifteen years old. It wasn't something that I had previously shared with him but I did tell my mom, albeit twenty-five years after the fact. The reason this information slipped by them was because when it occurred in 1971, I wasn't living at home with my parents. Like most relationships between parents and teenagers, we had issues; mine were specifically with my mother and unfortunately, they were serious issues.

As a young girl, I wasn't exactly happy with myself, particularly with the way I looked. I was a bit overweight and had bad skin. My mother, on the other hand, was absolutely gorgeous and multi-talented. She was popular and was often the center of attention, which she loved. I was a natural born introvert, and pretty much kept to myself. Not a day went by that I wasn't reminded of our differences. My mother's constant criticisms directed at me and my older sister were for the most part, downright cruel. Sadly, our emotional wounds festered. It's no mistake that my sister grew up to be a juvenile-psyche nurse. As for me, I was just lost.

So in an attempt to find the better, thinner me hidden inside a bigger girl's body, I went on a self-made diet. To avoid the disputes I had with my parents, I would go away for weeks at time during the summer months, sometimes even without their permission. I'd stay with friends and their parents because I felt they understood me better.

It wasn't that I was suicidal and had intentionally set out to kill myself; I just accidentally starved myself to death while trying to lose a few pounds. My "diet" had been going on for at least a year. Initially, it had seemed a good thing after the first ten pounds came off, but soon after, my parents realized that there was something else going on. A visit to the family doctor brought the diagnosis of anorexia and bulimia. I had never heard of these illnesses before and refused to accept that they applied to me because according to the doctor, these disorders were unhealthy. And I was convinced that I was doing a positive thing. After all, I was losing weight and that was what I had set out to do.

During the next few months, the doctor warned me that because of the rate I was losing the weight, I was putting myself in a life threatening situation. I was overworking my organs to the point where my heart could stop at any moment. Of course I didn't believe him; and even if it was a possibility, I rationalized it would only happen to someone else and not to me, which was a typical rationalization for an adolescent. My parents also had sent me to a psychologist, as per the doctor's recommendation; but this plan went nowhere fast because I was certain that it wasn't me with the problems. It was everyone else just making a big deal over "nothing". So I refused to do the work on my issues because in my mind, my low self-esteem came from being overweight rather than the other way around. Or should I say in *thinking* I was overweight. At this point, I had actually become quite thin, having lost 63 pounds, without even realizing it.

Due to my method of "dieting", I would often experience blackouts, which I never took too seriously. When I felt an episode coming on, I would just lower my head to get the blood flowing back into my brain again until the dizziness subsided. Then I would simply continue on with my day.

One afternoon, I was hanging out with two older boys who had just been introduced to me by high school friend. One of them was an acquaintance of her older brother. These two guys were high school pals who hadn't seen each other in a while and it happened that I was tagging along that day. We ended up at the beachfront home of one of the boys' parents. Suddenly, I felt myself blacking out again. It was very different this time because it felt as if my body was melting out from under me. To prevent myself from falling to the ground, I tried to inconspicuously grab onto the doorknob of the greenhouse that we were in, admiring homegrown orchids and marijuana plants. I didn't really know these guys since we had just met and didn't want to call attention to myself. My hope was that the feeling would pass as it had in the past. But it didn't happen that way this time. Almost immediately, I found myself floating above a lifeless, 85 pound body. What happened after that changed everything that I thought I knew about life.

It was a very confusing experience for me, because as I floated above my body, I was still able to think. At the time, I thought that thinking was a function of only the physical brain. I had no understanding of consciousness, or the spirit or even of what religious books referred to as "the soul." Although I had an inner knowingness of what was actually happening, I still couldn't totally comprehend whose body it was that I was looking down upon. At first I thought it was mine but then I wasn't sure because the girl I saw looked so sickly and emaciated, and that wasn't how I had ever seen myself. My perception was that I was fat, ugly and pimply faced. I watched puzzled as my new friends tried to revive "her" but it didn't look like they were having much luck. When I realized that there wasn't anything I could do to help her either, I hesitantly shifted my attention away from the befuddling site below me. And then it happened. I came face to face with the utmost brilliant and illuminating brightness – a radiant glow like I had never seen before! I was awestricken as it began pulsating in a most beautiful, synchronized dance around me. Its continuous motion seemed ready to sweep me up.

I quickly felt myself melding with the rhythm of the movement until I actually became a part of it. I had become one with the light! I had always felt like an outsider throughout my life. The glorious feeling of being a part of something—something bigger than me felt so safe and wonderful! At that point, I began to sense other beings around me and entered into a telepathic, two-way communication with them; they were asking me about the things that I hadn't done in my short lifetime and future dreams not yet accomplished. I can't say that at that age I had ever given much thought about a career choice or anything. According to the job listings in the newspaper, which I had scanned often, the only options I was aware of at the time for girls was to be a teacher, a secretary or nurse or the mysterious cad-key operator. I didn't even know what that was! All in all, I didn't think any of those goals were for me and dreamt only about that which I was sure of; moving away from my parent's house, getting my own apartment, marrying a nice man and having children. As I telepathically conveyed that thought to my questioners, it struck me, in that exact moment, that I would never get to see any unborn children who might have been destined for me…especially when I noticed that I could no longer see or even sense in any way, the physical body that had been left resting below me.

It was only then that I began to truly comprehend the extent of the situation I was in. The movement that had consumed me just moments before had gradually begun to dissipate somewhat, and as it diminished, the bright light softened. A multi-layered sadness crept through my being, sticking to the depths of my soul, leaving me feeling alone….and cheated. Why me, I wept. My tears, no longer physical, were of a vibrational nature that echoed through the heavens. How could this have happened? I just wanted to lose some weight, not all of my future dreams, simple as they were!

In my despair, a seed of hope must have sprouted, from where, I do not know, but I unexpectedly found myself embraced by what felt like loving arms cradling and rocking me, gently nurturing my soul. I was overcome by a sense of unconditional love, joy, and safety. And then most surprisingly, a feeling of *importance* encompassed me. Considering the low self-esteem that had tortured me for so long, valuable and important was not something that I was used to feeling. As I bathed in the awesomeness of this God-Light, I thought, "Wow, I could really get used to this! This is a good place for me to stay!"

Meanwhile, the beings of light chatted amongst themselves. I couldn't hear what they were saying but I somehow sensed that they were talking about me. I also sensed that they made a decision about something. All of a sudden there was a jolt and I found myself back in an empty, malnourished body that needed me to stay alive! I could feel the heart resume its beating while lifeblood traveled effortlessly through the roadways of the circulatory system. Then, as a slow, deep breath entered the lungs, I felt the chest rise, and I was aware of the oxygen circulating through the entire body that I soon recognized as mine. It has been said that the spirit enters the physical body on the first breath. It wasn't long before my other physical senses began to return. I noted the familiar aroma of the ocean. I could once again smell the salty air and hear with my physical ears the sounds of the waves crashing on the shore and the calls of seagulls nearby and in the distance. As I savored the familiar sounds, smells and tastes of the moment, I slowly opened my eyes and innately understood that all are gifts of God and most importantly, that there is a part of us that survives after physical death. I began to understand that the physical body just brings a different aspect to the totality of life. I also found that I had somehow absorbed information about other planes of reality that I had never known existed!

As I relayed to my father selective parts of my story, he listened politely as usual and then ended the conversation by calmly commenting, "An afterlife is one of those things that is just a mystery; no one really knows". I didn't press the issue with him. I just left it at that.

Chapter Two

"Why are you trying so hard to fit in when you were born to stand out?"
~ Ian Wallace

The fact that I had this opportunity to experience the spiritual realm as a teenager set me even further apart from other girls my age. I not only worried about my weight and wanting to fit in with the "in crowd", I now had to deal with the fact that I had discovered a part of myself that I didn't know I had, one that I couldn't even explain; a non-physical, spiritual part. I also knew that everyone had it, even if they didn't recognize it. I learned very quickly by trial and error that it wasn't something I should even try to discuss with anyone, not my sister, not my friends, my parents or cousins, because "normal" people just didn't speak of these things like finding oneself outside of the physical body and communicating with invisible spiritual beings. I so desperately wanted to fit in with my peers.

To say that I came back from that experience a bit changed is certainly a major understatement. Although I definitely had a new perspective on both life and what is known as death, I can't say that it was an experience that was easy for me to make sense of. But at the very least I had a new perception about this mystical place called "heaven". Coming to terms with what I thought I knew about "heaven" based on the religious classes I had attended in the past as opposed to what I experienced that summer afternoon, was to become a process that took many years for me to logically understand. I grappled with trying to find a balance between logic, which is what I thought the "normal" people based their lives on, and intuition and inner - knowingness, which is what I found myself depending on to guide my way.

Although I was raised as a Roman Catholic, we were not a family of devout church goers. After my sister, my brother and I went through the formalities of the receiving the sacraments of holy communion and confirmation, going to church was no longer in the family schedule, except for major Christian holidays like Christmas, Ash Wednesday and Easter. Probably we were hypocrites, as they say, but I think this was mostly due to the fact that our parents just couldn't come up with a good reason for attending church services that was compatible with what they actually believed, even though no one actually ever discussed what they believed. It simply never came up in a family discussion. We basically were taught that there most definitely is a God but we were left to define what that meant for ourselves. We were taught to live by the "golden rule" that we will "reap what we sow" and to treat others the way we wanted to be treated. The Ten Commandments also came into play on numerous occasions, so at the very least, we all developed a strong set of moral values.

As I look back at my childhood days, I was a very shy and quiet little girl. I recall always identifying with those who were considered different in some way; the kids who were less popular, the people who were pushed aside or looked down upon for one reason or another. It could be for reasons such as race, ethnic background, physical appearance or ability.

When I was twelve, I developed a pastime of visiting lonely seniors in a nearby nursing home. This first began as a Girl Scout project that matched scouts with "adoptive grandparents" -- a program that I played a large part in launching in an effort to earn a badge that was to decorate my new scout uniform and sash that my beautiful, talented, thin and perfectly figured mom had made for me. Oh, how I yearned to look like her! But interestingly, each time I stepped into that urine scented building, I forgot all about my insecurities. I had a knack for seeing beyond the outward appearances of others, and connecting on a spiritual level, particularly incapacitated, drooling old people.

Little did I know at the time that this new "hobby" of mine, which I believe had sprung from the core of my true self, would years later, end up reclaiming my heart long after I was assaulted by the uncertainties of adolescence, the need to fit in and to be accepted by others who were more popular than I was.

In the next several decades after my near death experience, my interests gradually gravitated in the direction of learning everything I could about the transition from life to death. I came to view this phase of life as a holy and sacred time. I spent many long hours researching what was written about the mysteries of the afterlife and about other unexplainable metaphysical activity to see if any of it was similar to what I had experienced. At the same time I also set out to define and better understand my own spirituality. During this period I came to realize that I possessed in a deep place within me, a multifaceted connection to what I viewed as God's constant action in my life. I also developed a faith and trust so strong that I became certain that whatever internal suffering I had previously faced in my past, or for that matter, whatever I might face in the future, actually would have opportunities for my own growth hiding behind it.

Over the years as my own extended family members, neighbors and friends began to face terminal illness and death; my near death experience remained crystal clear in my mind as if it had just happened. And because it was such a beautiful and remarkable experience for me, death itself wasn't something that I personally feared or worried about too much. However, I did realize that the process of dying is a scary journey and believed that no one should ever have to embark upon that journey alone.

As a matter of fact, studies have shown that for most people, dying is the number one thing in life that people fear the most. According to research, much of this fear stems from simply not knowing what happens after the physical body dies. That's when it occurred to me that because of my experience with the "other side", I might be able to make a difference in the lives of people who were facing death. I could do this by sharing my own story or possibly, I could at least guide them through the process of accepting one's own life story and being okay with it in an effort to reduce their fear and anxiety. And then I learned about Hospice.

According to the National Hospice and Palliative Care Organization (NHPCO), the hospice philosophy affirms all aspects of life and exists to provide support and care for those in the last stages of medically incurable illness so that they might live out the remainder of their lives as fully and as comfortably as possible. Hospice recognizes dying as a normal process whether or not it results from disease. Hospice care neither hastens nor postpones death, allowing a person to die when the time naturally comes, rather than trying to keep him/her alive on machines or through resuscitation. Hospice programs do not generally include surgery, routine intravenous therapy or blood transfusions, nor place people on respirators, unless one of these procedures could relieve pain and make the patient more comfortable. Hospice exists in the hope and belief that, through appropriate care and the promotion of a caring community that is sensitive to their needs, patients and families may be free to attain a degree of mental and spiritual preparation for death that is satisfactory to them. Additionally, hospice works with the whole family, not just the person who is ill, and supports both the patients and their families in making the major decisions about a program of care. Support continues to be offered to the family even after the death of the patient.

I decided that the hospice philosophy is one that I truly could support so I enrolled myself in a local hospice volunteer training program.

After completing my training and visiting with clients, I discovered another thing that people also fear regarding the subject of death; and that is to actually spend time with someone who is dying. One of the reasons for this is that caregivers and visitors oftentimes find themselves struggling with their own fears about dying, death and loss, which ends up making them very uncomfortable being with someone who is facing it..

When someone we love is dying, we too, begin a tortuous journey. We begin to feel the pain of loss in every aspect of ourselves; the emotional, physical, mental and spiritual. I had come to realize that these components of self are not separate from one another; they are completely intertwined even though in different situations we might focus on one aspect more than another.

Seeing someone who is terminally ill, particularly after their body has begun to significantly deteriorate, is very difficult for most people to accept and deal with, especially if the deterioration is to the point where the person we once knew is almost unrecognizable. This is a scenario that most people dread.

In many cases, even though we may want to be there for our loved one and may even feel that we "should" be available to them, it is not unusual to try and talk ourselves out of it, knowing that the emotional pain would be too agonizing. The stress of seeing a loved one facing death can cause feelings of physical sickness, such as headache, nausea, upset stomach or even tightening or pains to the chest. I have learned as a hospice volunteer that for the most part, terminal patients are fully aware of the uneasiness that their illness can have on their friends and family, resulting in them feeling sad and maybe even guilty for their visitors' discomfort. It can take a lot of courage on everyone's part to open the mind and move past the awkwardness of these circumstances. And as I have found, it could certainly be well worth the effort.

Thinking back to my Girl Scout days and visits with the nursing home residents, the only way I was able to see beyond a patient's deteriorating physical appearance was to view them from the eyes of my heart or, in other words, from a spiritual perspective. I did that by just momentarily stepping out from any fearful emotions I may have had, and calming myself just long enough to allow my love to merge with his/her love. Then when the deepest part of me connected with the deepest part of my patient, it would bring forth a sacred and eternal connection, one that was able to carry and guide both of us over the bumpy parts of the journey. This is the merging of souls, the blending of two Spirits.

One of the things that attracted me to hospice is that the hospice model treats all aspects of a person; the physical, emotional, mental and spiritual. Throughout my life I had become very familiar with how these very different parts of our being are intertwined and how they complement and work with each and every other part as a whole. I understood that these different parts are all forms of energy that are simply vibrating at different frequencies and ideally, should function in harmony together. My favorite metaphor for this concept is that of a clock face where the slowly moving hour hand gives us one piece of information, while the faster moving minute hand gives us another piece of information. The secondhand, moving faster than the two other hands offers us even more detail about the time whilst all hands are part of the same face. When working properly, one component does not work without the others.

I discovered that with each hospice assignment I took, I learned a little bit more about myself in the process. Each self-discovery provided me with a straighter path to my own spirituality. I found, just as others who have also been called to this type of work have found, that as we gave fully and freely to others from an open heart the love that was given would always find its way back to us. It has caused me to fully understand that we truly are all one. One of my favorite quotes:

> *"The humanity in each of us is ultimately dependent on recognizing the humanity in all of us."*
> Author unknown

I believe that as a hospice volunteer, I had actually been helped by my patients just as much as, if not more than, how much I helped them! It is no wonder that the meaning of the word "hospice", which come comes from the Latin term "hospes", is defined as both host and guest.

THE TWILIGHT BRIGADE

After about a year as a hospice volunteer serving several clients, I was introduced to an organization called *"The Twilight Brigade"* (formerly known as *"Compassion in Action")*. *The Twilight Brigade* is a national, non-profit organization dedicated to both educating people about death and dying and to recruiting and training volunteers for hospice, with the goals of placing them in existing hospice and volunteer programs in nursing homes, hospitals and hospices throughout the United States.

The Twilight Brigade's training program can either stand alone or complement other hospice training programs. Different than other programs, the Twilight Brigade offers an additional training component which consists of a series of experiential exercises that were designed to all build on one another and encourage the trainees to confront and resolve their own fears about death, dying and loss so that they can better serve those who are facing it.

After completing this 20 hour course I began serving as a *Twilight Brigade* bedside volunteer in a local nursing home in addition to my hospice assignments from the other Connecticut facility of which I was associated. This gave me a great deal of experience in end of life care. I learned that the need for this kind of volunteering was especially great due to the fact that families of nursing home residents often lived far away from their loved ones and cannot easily make regular visits. After a few years of trying to divide my time between dozens of nursing home residents, not all of whom were actively dying but received huge benefit from a visit, I thought it would be ideal to have more people doing it. That's when I formed the Connecticut affiliate of the *Twilight Brigade* so that I could facilitate trainings and build a team of volunteers in my area to help serve this often overlooked portion of the population. I feel that the dying time is a very important and sacred part of life. We will all be there some day, either as a patient or caregiver, so to me it made complete sense to help people learn how to be more comfortable in that role.

Chapter Three

"The future has a way of arriving unannounced."
~ George Will

AT THIS POINT in my life I had become an experienced hospice volunteer, familiar with and interested in the many aspects of death and dying. I was very proud of how far I had come on my spiritual journey through life, often giving lectures and presentations about what I had learned from my NDE and sharing my story with people at various conferences and group talks along the east coast. I loved the fact that so many people had become openly interested in such esoteric topics. I was also very proud of my volunteer work with hospice. I felt blessed to be able to intimately connect to perfect strangers during what is often the scariest time of their lives.

On a personal level, things seemed to be going quite well for me. It was midsummer, a quiet, warm evening in 2005. I had just returned from a conference in Orlando where I had given a talk about "Heaven". It was based entirely on my own experiences dealing with what I learned as a result of my NDE, as well as from my continued lifelong communications with the Light Beings I had encountered in those realms. Over the years I had routinely met with them while in a meditative state to seek answers to esoteric questions about life, death and beyond. This particular conference was important to me because the information that I presented jibed with various scientific explanations of mystical experiences presented by other speakers in the scientific community. My presentation was also compatible with personal information described by others who, like me, had also been blessed to visit the "other side" and come back to talk about it. All in all, as I shared how these planes relate to us in this life and in the "hereafter", I felt that my presentation was well received by those who had attended the conference.

Switching gears and back at home, I had settled into the daily routines of a busy work day, the responsibilities of parenting and household chores. By this time in my life, I had been blessed with three children to raise. My oldest son, Rashid, had recently graduated from college and was living and working in North Carolina. My daughter, Saida, was a student at the University of Connecticut. She lived on campus but came home on weekends to work at her part-time job. My youngest son, Hassan, was a teenager struggling to find his place in the world. My husband and I had been married for seventeen years but grew apart and were divorced eight years before.

After cooking a simple meal, I looked forward to my favorite time of day -- dessert time. I typically relax after dinner with a freshly-brewed cup of coffee coupled with a blissful piece of deliciousness. On this day, I took pleasure in eating the spicy, moist sweetness of a bakery-style supermarket carrot cake that was covered in rich cream cheese icing. Needless to say, it quickly excited my taste buds. Meanwhile, I reflected on a day that had gone relatively well. My daughter was working at her summer job while home from college. Her younger brother, who had always been quite a handful, often stayed with his father and was not expected home with me on that particular day. The calm of the moment was particularly appreciated. I had a feeling it wouldn't last long though, so I did my best to soak in as much enjoyment from my cake and solitude for as long as possible. But unfortunately, my carrot cake-induced paradise lasted only a few brief moments when the sound of the phone jingled nearby.

As I glanced at the caller ID, I could see that it was my sister who was calling. In those days it seemed that she frequently was the bearer of not-so-good news. So, pausing a moment, I consciously made an effort to brace myself before answering. Donna was the nurse in the family and could speak from a clinical perspective about medical issues, so in addition to being the oldest, I believe that was why she was the one chosen to break the news.

And sure enough, the news wasn't good. Our father had received test results that showed a strong possibility of pancreatic cancer; but because it was not yet one hundred percent conclusive, there would be no treatment until more was known. Although my father had had a series of relatively minor health issues over the previous few years, he was actually feeling quite well, except for the fact that in recent months he had been slowly and consistently losing weight. Even though it brought him some concern he didn't advertise the fact, at least not to me.

He did, however, admit to having days when he was emotionally drained from caring for my mother, who, for the previous four years, had been suffering from post-herpetic neuralgia due to an extreme case of shingles that wasn't treated in time. The shingles was triggered when she learned that her younger sister was diagnosed with a brain tumor. The stress of the news brought the painful rash that had covered her head, face and neck. The pain killers prescribed were not working and so the doses and strengths increased steadily over time. My mother's life changed considerably in a downward direction. In addition to that, fourteen years since losing his only sibling to lung cancer, my father had been solely responsible for the care of his own father, who, at a healthy one hundred years old, had left this earth due only to old age just a few weeks before on Rashid's twenty-fifth birthday.

If the diagnosis was found to be positive, my father would be the first immediate family member to become terminally ill since I had become a hospice volunteer ten years earlier.

Upon hearing the news, I was totally shocked since I had not been aware that he had been dealing with something so serious. Like an erupting volcano, a sudden avalanche of anxieties exploded through my head, momentarily paralyzing the lobes of my brain and leaving me speechless. Then my own fearful thoughts quickly overpowered my sister's words as she relayed the worst case scenarios. Even though there was a disconnect between me and her words, we both became emotional at the exact same time. We wept together, sobbing until our eyes ran dry of tears. I hadn't been ready for so much emotion. It caught me completely off guard. I scrambled for something positive to hang onto to reverse the swelling sensation that had entered my brain and heart. "Since we don't know for sure, I remember saying calmly, "I will hope and pray for the best". I remained stunned as I hung up the phone, and I knew I would be calling my dad, but first I needed some time to gather my thoughts.

This new "opportunity", the possible chance to join my father on his journey through the last phases of his life on this earth, was not one to which I looked forward to. I imagined that it would be a journey very different from those I had shared with hospice clients. This time, I would not only be a caregiver, but also a daughter. I wondered if I be able to be an effective caregiver for my father during this precious time, especially when I knew that I would also be needing comfort. How would I cope with the barrage of feelings that were sure to come up? I was suddenly thrust into a world of unknowns. I need to put some safety measures in place, I thought. And with that, I quickly made an effort to position myself on the edge of denial in the event I needed a quick and temporary escape from the reality of the moment. Even my carrot cake could no longer soothe me.

By the time my finger dialed the phone number that I had memorized since I was four years old, I had focused my mind on hope for a good outcome. Whether this meant my father would be cured of the disease or whether he would have what is referred to as a "good death". According to an Institute of Medicine report, a good death is one that is *"Free from avoidable distress and suffering for the patient, family and caregivers, in general accord with the patient's and family's wishes, and reasonably consistent with clinical, cultural and ethical standards."*

My Dad had always been a chronic worrier and had spent his lifetime keeping his emotional burdens inside until he could create opportunities to hammer them out whilst in the process of building additions on the house, or some other construction project. Although I didn't know it then, my father's larger projects helped him get through the stress of dealing with my teenage years. But at this point in time, the house was big enough and there was no more need for another building project, nor did he have the strength or motivation for such undertakings.

When I heard his voice, I was surprised that my father, too, outwardly expressed the same thought process that I had after talking to Donna, which was to try and stay positive and hope for the best. But it was almost spooky how relaxed and accepting he sounded about this new development with his health. He calmly went on to tell me that he would deal with it by living one day at a time until he knew more about it.

He also said he was making it a point to keep himself busy. He was feeling relatively good, still golfing with his friends, tackling the household chores and trying to keep my mother comfortable. Before hanging up the phone, I had promised to visit soon.

Chapter Four

*"An open ear is the only believable
sign of an open heart."*
~ David Augsburger

For the first time since I could remember, and I think by the grace of God, my dad and I were getting positioned to meet each other soul to soul. Although I could easily describe the both of us as deep thinkers, I can't say that our profound thinking processes had ever led to a deep communication between us. I guessed that it would be sooner rather than later that we would find ourselves having just such a conversation, presumably about the realities and nuances of life and death.

My father had known about my work with hospice and my interest in end of life care but like many of the other people in my life, it wasn't a subject most of them wanted to hear about, or much less talk about. Lighter conversation was generally more comfortable for my family, so as a result, I would normally keep that part of me to myself, especially when I was with family members

Even though my NDE was in 1971, it had only been 8 years before receiving my father's news when I finally told my mom about it. On that occasion, we were riding on the Metro-North to New York City to attend a lecture by Dannion Brinkley about his amazing near-death experience which was depicted in his book and the movie "Saved by the Light". Somehow we had gotten on the subject of my troubled teenage years, which had been a living hell for the whole family, when I finally shared what had happened to me. Although my focus in sharing was the part about my mystical experience, my mother was focused on the part about her teenaged daughter lying there dead. "We were so afraid that you would die", my mother sobbed, trying unsuccessfully to hold back the tears, her makeup smudging her face. "The doctor told us it could happen at any time but the things we tried to do to help you just didn't work. We were left feeling helpless to do anything about it." A lapse in the conversation gave my mother a moment to compose herself, as other passengers on the train nonchalantly tried not to notice the emotional display she was trying to be discreet about. After regaining composure she continued, "I'm glad we didn't know back then that our biggest fear actually did come true", she reasoned. "We never would have been able to deal with it".

Looking back to that day on the train, I realized that my mother hadn't ever told my father what had happened. She probably decided that some things are better left hidden.

With my hospice patients, I had always been careful not to bring up my own personal brush with death unless the patient brought up the subject first in some way. I had learned that it is most important to meet the patients where they are and leave your own agenda at the door. More often than not, where they are is struggling to deal with their own life issues, so interjecting one's own story would be inappropriate.

The day had arrived for my first visit with my dad after his news was broken. It started out as an ordinary day in terms of our conversation. I gave him updates on his grandchildren, talked about work related topics, and how my car was running. I will admit that I was secretly hoping we would be able to get into something more substantial like the meaning of life or what might be waiting for us after death. But I came to learn that it would take many small steps to reach that juncture in a natural way.

Up until that point, I hadn't realized the seriousness of my mother's condition until my father opened up and talked about the day to day challenges he faced regarding her illness and her care. Although she had been in constant and excruciating pain for four years, she had always done an excellent job at hiding it from the rest of us. The fact that our family gatherings had become more infrequent and my mother typically was not a complainer, her real truth was easily kept hidden. But now that I was there on a regular day, rather than a holiday, I witnessed something very abnormal. My mother was brought to an expressionless state of unconsciousness by the large doses of pain killers that her doctor had prescribed, making her appear as if she had joined the living dead. Aside from the fact that it was painful and tragic for me to see that my vibrant, vivacious mother had been reduced to this demoralizing condition, it was even more heart-wrenching to see the pain in my father's eyes for her. I could easily understand why he wasn't focusing on his own health issues.

Each subsequent visit with my parents showed increasing decline in my mother's condition. She had seen every specialist in the area and tried everything that was recommended including the implantation of an electrical nerve stimulation device. Unfortunately, soon after the device was inserted, it became infected and damaged the nerves even more, leaving my mother in even worse pain than before, after it was removed. Her case quickly became complicated due to her previously diagnosed heart disease. I tried to encourage a holistic approach such as herbal and energy therapies to relieve some of her pain, but mom resisted change and unfortunately, was still hoping to find the perfect pill.

In a totally different way than I had expected, the subject of death finally did come up. During one particular visit, Dad appeared especially worried. In an attempt to find out what he was thinking, I asked him what he thought might happen with mom's illness. His eyes welled up as he blurted out that he thought she might die. The thought of her dying was more than he could take. To compound the issue, his fears about his own possible illness began to bubble to the surface, exposing his anxiety about the possibility of no longer being able to care for his wife. It had been difficult for him while he was healthy, never mind trying to do it while sick. My father's worries were etched deeply into his face. His whole body hung limp. "I don't know what I will do if I'm in as much pain as she is," my dad ruminated, "because I don't think I have the tolerance or the determination that your mother has to live everyday like that. "We will work it out", I said quietly.

A man's man, my father could only talk about his feelings in small doses. A few sentences were all he could handle. I took the cue and left him alone while I tidied up in the kitchen and tended to my mother.

When I joined him again in the living room, I planted myself on the couch beside him. "Karin." he said, almost in a whisper, "I was just thinking while you were busy with your mother, about when you were younger. I just want you to know that I didn't always agree how she treated you girls, but we vowed to keep a united front, at least when we were in the same room with you kids. What do you think the main problem was between you two; when the eating disorder developed?" "I think I was envious and jealous of her beauty and talents", I answered, without even pausing to think about it, and then added, "aside from the fact that she always made it a point to make me feel like crap".

After taking in a deep breath, he held it inside his lungs and closed his eyes while slowly shaking his head back and forth "I knew it" my father said softly, probably remembering every conversation he had had with his wife on the subject "I always told her you were jealous and she adamantly disagreed every time. "NO, that can't be", she would tell me. I also thought she was cruel in some ways but she insisted her methods would build character and motivate you to do better." "Well, I can't say that her cruelty motivated me in any way other than to find a way to get out of the house as soon as possible", I responded, my words trailing off into a whisper as I finished the sentence. I was gradually overpowered by some horrible memories. At that particular moment, we purposely put an abrupt end to that part of the conversation because my dad's daily emotional quota had already been met earlier in the day, and anyway, I didn't feel like talking about that topic either. I preferred to end on a positive note; I wanted him to know about the defining day in my life when my trajectory suddenly changed. It was the first time I had shared what had taken place when my heart came to a stop on that summer day thirty-three years earlier. And a very good listener my father was…

Chapter Five

Life is lived forward but it is understood backward"
- Soren Kierkegaard

The subject of death may come up easily for those who are healthy but for those who aren't well and are facing the end of life due to terminal illness or some other tragic event; it can be a very awkward topic to bring up. But no matter how uncomfortable it may be, it still is a subject that terminally ill people think about even when they are pretending that life is going on as usual as to not upset their loved ones. For this reason, they will often welcome someone bringing up the white elephant in the room first. If you catch the hint and if that someone is you, what should you say? And how should you say it?

Talking about life is often a good lead-in to talking about

death. Reminiscing about past events often helps to create a trusting and safe environment which can strengthen existing bonds with your loved one or even create new ones. Revisiting life stories, whether happy or sad, and recapturing the feelings associated with those events can help in sorting out unresolved issues. A life review can be an empowering tool because it has a way of stabilizing the past so that the present can be more accepted and embraced. This ultimately can help to make any fears that are lurking around about facing the future feel less daunting.

As you and your loved one share your stories and become fully present in the moment, it can provide a safe space to attempt to find out their thoughts about end of life topics. You can ask them, as I did in reference to my mom, "What do you think might happen with your illness?" You may be surprised by the multiple responses that this question can bring up. It can expose vulnerabilities, fears and aspects of them that may have previously been kept hidden. It can also open up moments of grace and beauty as both life and death are acknowledged.

There are numerous losses a terminally ill person must face either gradually as the illness progresses or in some cases, all at once. Some of the more obvious losses are those that deal with the physical aspects of life and can range from losing the ability to do physical activities that were once loved and enjoyed or to the more mundane, such as tending to one's own daily care such as eating, bathing and toileting. Decreasing mobility that can result in the need to use a cane, wheel chair or walker may also be quite upsetting for the patient and difficult to accept. And for many people, coming to the realization that driving is no longer an option for them is often distressful as well. Sometimes just the anticipation of such life changes can cause mental anguish and be both terrifying and depressing.

In addition to the physical aspects of loss, worrying about losing the ability to make one's own choices and decisions can bring distress, along with concerns about one's changing roles within the family, especially if they are someone who has always been in a position to take care of others. This can create additional anxiety about who will care for and support their survivors after they are gone. Additionally, there can be angst over what might happen to any prized possessions that carry sentimental value or questions like "What will my legacy be and how might it be celebrated?"

Coping with loss is one of life's biggest challenges. It is a uniquely personal experience for those going through it. Although no one can truly understand everything that their loved one may be dealing with physically, emotionally and spiritually during a time of loss or even during a time of anticipated loss, just having someone there can bring comfort to the process. Grief and loss are often best dealt with by simply allowing it to be felt and experienced. If you can create a safe space for your loved one without trying to fix anything or by making judgements, it can be a great comfort on this difficult journey.

Oftentimes, just allowing the patient to talk about their distress will give them some relief from it, because by making verbal statements aloud, it creates an opportunity for them to acknowledge their pain. Acknowledgment is the first step in accepting the reality of a painful situation. In so doing, it will put them in a position to begin healing. If, on the other hand, a person attempts to resist the pain that their grief brings, it will only prolong the natural process of healing.

In addition to what I just mentioned, one of my dad's biggest fears was of being in pain. Pancreatic cancer is known to bring excruciating pain, which fortunately, up to that point, he didn't seem to be experiencing. However, we all routinely asked him about it anyway. One day, after I popped the question, my father didn't give his normal response of "not yet" but allowed his worried pupils to lock onto mine. It seemed like he was staring straight through my eyeballs to the point where his gaze penetrated my eye sockets. I was instantly pulled into his world and could actually feel his deep anguish weighing heavy on my spirit. "Does emotional pain count?" he whispered. I was glad that I was there for him at that moment.

All you need to do is to be fully present and to listen. The patience, tolerance and love that an open heart requires can be the most intimate and compassionate action that you can offer to your loved one.

Chapter Six

*"There is no one giant step that does
it. It's a lot of little steps."*
~ Author Unknown

My next visit home brought an opportune time to introduce my dad to my work as a holistic health practitioner. My specialty is energy healing and over the years had become a very important part of who I am, although, unfortunately, it was another part of my life that other family members didn't seem to have an interest in. I was hoping that my father might be open to hearing about it now that he had a reason to learn about all options open to him

My near-death experience had given me a basic insight into the workings of the heavenly realms within the "multi-verse" which is made up of everything that exists: the totality of space, time, matter, energy, and the physical laws and constants that describe them. This led me to a deep interest in learning to utilize this energy system to promote positive changes in the physical body. Scientists and energy healers alike have known for centuries that we have an energetic component to ourselves that surrounds, interpenetrates and interacts with our physical body. Energy Healing is a spiritually guided approach to healing that manipulates, restores and balances the flow of subtle energies around and through us. The energy is then channeled through the practitioner's physical body to be released to the client's energy field. The energy body, also known by some as "chi" comes into a state of re-alignment and is brought back into a place of harmony. This creates an environment for the emotional and physical aspects of ourselves to begin to selfheal. When the re-alignment occurs, it is the perfect time to identify and work through longtime, unresolved emotional issues because eliminating emotional stresses will greatly affect the physical body in a positive way.

An ancient Japanese healing technique known as *Reiki*, as well as other methods of energy healing such as *laying-on of hands*, which is often a part of many religious practices; or the science based *therapeutic touch* which was introduced to western medical science by Dolores Kreiger; the *pranic healing* of eastern traditions and countless others, have been effective in helping virtually every known illness and malady. Energy Healing has been known to always create some kind of beneficial effect, whether mental, emotional, physical or spiritual. Energy healing methods have been proven to work in conjunction with all other medical or therapeutic techniques to relieve side effects and promote recovery.

For this reason in recent decades, hospitals and medical facilities all over the world have begun incorporating Reiki, which is currently the most popular energy healing method, into their treatment plans as an option for those who agree to use it.

I was thrilled when dad asked again about my near-death experience and wanted more details about it. In that first conversation, I was very careful not to bombard him with too many paranormal elements of the event out of fear of turning him away. I had so much to share about the invisible world of Spirit and I was sure that it would, in some way, be really helpful to him. So this time I took an even bigger risk. I began by explaining that while on the "other side" I realized that "Heaven" isn't actually a "place", but an entire *system* – a system of subtle energies that are constantly stirring about, and are magnetically attracting other energy forms, commonly known as the law of attraction. In addition to that, (even though I figured it would be difficult for him to imagine and accept), I went on to describe how these subtle energies are often gently manipulated with the assistance of invisible energy beings, such as the ones I had encountered during my near-death experience. These beings, like us, are energetically entwined with the Divine Source of all creation and love, (also known as the God consciousness) and help to create new effects that facilitate shaping and transforming our daily lives. I was so excited sharing this with him! It felt as though I had finally come out of a spiritual closet that allowed me to expose one of the miracles of the universe that had influenced my life-long attitudes and lifestyle! At that point, I didn't care whether or not he believed what I was telling him, or even if he thought I was nut case, just that he remembered it for future reference. So I continued talking and shared with my father how I had eventually become a certified Reiki practitioner. While in training, I was taught the physical mechanics of what was required of me as a practitioner, but because of my NDE, I was also aware that there was a lot happening on the spiritual planes that was invisible to the human eye. The invisible part is the exciting part because it is the part that makes all methods of energy healing work. I knew that unseen spirit beings (whom I like to call God's helpers) work as a team with the practitioner by manipulating and blending the subtle energies together. They dilute any negative energy contained in the mix by utilizing the energy of divine, pure love from the Divine Source. It's as if new "energy recipes" are created from existing ingredients within the "chi" to bring about a positive change in the receiver's energetic body. The new positively charged energy forms are then channeled through the practitioner's energy field and then flow through his/her hands to ultimately affect the client in a positive way on a cellular level.

Clinical studies have shown evidence that energy healing *does* work but not *how* it works. Science is still working on that. For years as a Reiki practitioner, I would often pray to God, asking if there was a way to help clients to understand what happens *invisibly* during the energy healing treatment. Of course, during the treatment, the practitioner's actions are in plain view in the physical world, but because I knew that this is only part of the process, I kept on praying. I was well aware that perhaps, I was asking for a tall order in wanting my clients to witness a phenomenon, but that didn't stop me; I have always believed in miracles anyway!

Over the years, numerous scientific studies have been conducted on the subject of energy healing. Dr. Daniel J. Benor, MD, ABIHM compiled and published many of these studies in his book entitled *"Healing Research",* which contains three volumes. He has also published numerous articles on holistic and spiritual healing. In one such study conducted at the Helfgott Research Institute at the national college of Naturopathic medicine in Portland Oregon, it was shown that energy healing has a measurable effect on the immune system by increasing the number of white cells in those who received the treatment. Another study has demonstrated its ability to increase hemoglobin values significantly in patients diagnosed with a wide range of illnesses including pancreatitis, brain tumor, emphysema, multiple endocrine disorders, rheumatoid arthritis, and congestive heart failure.

According to researchers in St Louis, Missouri, energy healing can inhibit the growth of tumors and is therefore a worthwhile complementary therapy for cancer patients. The researchers investigated the effect of energy healing upon tumor cell growth in a laboratory. An energy healer was selected to give healing energy to cancer cells (in vitro). These cells were then compared with similar cancer cells which were not exposed to the healer and left in a room set at the same temperature and same lighting conditions.

The results showed that the healing energy did have a significant influence on the rate of growth of the tumor cells. Compared to the control group of cells, the cancer cells exposed to healing energy showed inhibited growth.

In their paper, "The Healing Presence: Can it be Reliably Measured?" Wayne Jonas, MD and Cindy Crawford, BA discuss "what healers from various traditions have felt are the primary components of a healing presence, summarizes various attempts to measure healing, and describes two recently published approaches that have potential to provide such and objective and real time indicator of *a healing presence*."

This is just an example of some of the studies that were conducted on the subject. I, however, became more excited about the miracle that eventually revealed itself in regards to a healing presence!

Finally, several years and many prayers later, I discovered that my prayers had been answered! I had been blessed with a way to actually show people some of what is happening invisibly "behind the veil".

I had often offered Reiki sessions to nursing home residents. One day, while working with a gentleman in a local nursing home facility, I suddenly felt an odd sensation coming over me.

As this occurred, my hands began making deliberate and specific motions in the airspace above the man's body, moving by themselves, without any voluntary action from me! The movements were precise and methodical. Both my client and I were in a state of pleasant amazement, as it was obvious that my hands were moving by a force that was separate from me! Then I perceived an audible voice from the heaven-space around me, "Why are you so surprised? Isn't this what you have been asking for? This is *Aiijii Healing*, a melding of the physical with the spiritual".

I had never heard of Aiijii Healing before, it was a new term that was given to me from the heavenly planes. In Aiijii Healing, non-physical heavenly beings (known to me as "Healing Guides"), blend their own energy bodies into the energy field of the practitioner, enabling them to 'borrow" the practitioner's body and physically move the hands to manipulate and blend energies together. This allows the client to actually see the normally invisible Spirit activity during an energy healing treatment. The Aiijii method of healing gives people a concrete way to have a Spiritual understanding of healing by giving them a glimpse of what is going on in the invisible realm of spirit. The effects of any energy healing treatment will speak for itself.

This demonstrative healing method utilizes the expression "Seeing is Believing" and interestingly, supports the findings gathered in a randomized clinical trial by Raymond F Palmer and his colleagues. Their aim was to "investigate the relevance of interpersonal belief factors as modifiers of the effectiveness of intercessory prayer" on a variety of health outcomes. They found that the results of their study "underscore the role of interpersonal belief in prayer efficacy and are consistent with the literature showing the relevance that belief has in health and well-being in general."

While watching the "Healing Guides" work, people are reminded of the miracles that can occur when there is complete faith and trust in God. I have found it to be humbling to witness how we, in the physical world, work with those in the spiritual realm to bring about energetic changes that create emotional changes that can then materialize into physical changes.

From that day on, I became known as an Aiijii Practitioner, rather than a Reiki Practitioner. I think it's worth mentioning that all energy healing methods work the same way; that is, the spiritual team does their part of manipulating energy and the practitioner acts as a conduit to complete the delivery.

As I mentioned previously, there are numerous energy healing methods being used all over the world. No one particular method is "better" than another. The energetic makeup of the spiritual teams requires specific compatibility with the energetic makeup of the individual practitioners with whom they partner with. They work together in the most energetically efficient way possible, using the method or methods that are intuitively comfortable for the practitioner. In all cases and methods, it is the communion or attunement to the Divine Source that is the miracle.

My father listened patiently to everything I had to say and then in a decision based on a combination of desperation, intrigue and respect for me and my work, he decided to give Aiijii healing a try.

Following the first treatment, he described feeling calmer and comforted as if "a bubble of love had engulfed him". In addition to that, he spoke of a warming sensation during the session that left him less anxious and more relaxed both during the session and afterward. Happy with the results thus far, he agreed to set up regularly scheduled sessions every other day. When I wasn't physically at his house, I would administer the healing over the phone. He would lie comfortably in his bed or on the couch with the phone on speaker beside him. I played a CD of soothing music for him to listen to while we (the healing team and I) worked. Based on a series of studies, energy healing treatments administered over the phone or skype across time and space have proven to be quite effective. Over the coming months my father waited by the phone at the appointed time for my call. I began to feel a bond with him growing that I had not known before.

Chapter Seven

"Sometimes you need a little crisis to get your adrenaline flowing and help you realize your potential."
~ Jeannette Walls, The Glass Castle

AFTER DEALING WITH doctors on vacation, and a series of more inconclusive tests, it was late fall before the final verdict was in. Again, it was my sister who called and broke the news about the dreaded positive diagnosis of cancer. Even though I had been seeing my father more often in the past months and our relationship had grown, we had still gradually reverted to our old patterns of light, surface conversation. But now with this news, I was feeling an immediate urgency for us to get to know each other better. There were so many things I didn't know about him and so many things he didn't know about me. Growing up, I hadn't really shared a lot with him, such as my hopes and dreams or my passions and beliefs. It's not that he didn't want to try to connect with me, my mother recently explained to me in one of her moments of clarity, he just didn't know how to. Throughout my childhood as a natural born introvert, I normally stayed in my own private world, afraid to come out or to let others in. But now as an adult, I had become more trusting of the world around me and comfortable in my own skin. It's now or never, I thought to myself, but what would I say? I wondered. Where would I begin? And *how* would I begin?"

As a facilitator of hospice trainings, the question I was most often asked by others is what *does* one say to a dying person? But now I was asking myself, what does one say to a father who had just been positively diagnosed with a terminal illness? A father to whom one had, for the last thirty something years, only seen on holidays and at family gatherings in group situations? A father who was *my* father and whose diagnosis was pancreatic cancer that was deemed inoperable and known to grow quickly and produce excruciating pain? The thought of death itself was not the problem for me, but imagining my father in the pain that he feared the most and losing him prematurely when we were just beginning to bond, was certainly a big problem.

After several months of imagining different scenarios and hoping and praying for the best, the reality of the news was finally beginning to sink in. It was harder now to stay on the edge of denial because deep in my gut, I knew that it was true. How could this be happening to him? How could this be happening to us, as a family? And even selfishly, how can this be happening to *me*? All of this just isn't fair. My parents' lives had changed so much already because of mom's current health limitations and now my father, her main caregiver, would soon be needing care himself. They both had always been very independent, active and relatively healthy, How would my sister, brother and I, as a unit, deal with two very sick parents? I also couldn't help wondering if there would be any deeply buried, unresolved family issues that would come up between us during this ordeal to complicate matters, as I had regularly seen in other families I had dealt with. Suppressed, unresolved issues always seem to ooze to the surface in a time of crisis which, in itself is not necessarily a bad thing as long as these things are addressed properly as soon as they come up. Just the thought of compounding emotions from the past with those in the present was sounding overwhelming to me. Even aside from those concerns, there were so many other things to work out. The logistics alone would be tricky.

I lived fifty miles away from our home town, my sister seventy-five miles. Together with our work and family schedules, I knew this wouldn't be easy. Although my younger brother had settled his family within minutes of our childhood home, my sister and I didn't want to leave him and his wife with the brunt of the day to day responsibilities of caregiving and running a second household. I knew that this was often the case in other families whose geographic location prevented the equal sharing of family duties.

My siblings and I felt a family meeting was called for and

during that meeting decided that we would each initially contribute one or two days a week to help dad with mom as needed. This action would be new not only to our parents, but also to us because we had always been a family that prided ourselves on independence; always determined to work through our challenges by ourselves. We normally shared our trials and tribulations with each other only after we were on track again. It wasn't that we were afraid to ask each other for help. I like to think it was more that we respected each other's busy schedules and didn't want to feel we were burdening each other. However, more realistically, I can admit that our egos and pride also played a part of that, too, which allowed us some stubbornness. But no matter what had influenced our decisions in the past, this situation was different now because our parents' need for support would not only be emotional; it would be physical, too.

Since Dad's tumor was inoperable due to its location amongst veins and arteries, he chose an aggressive treatment plan of several rounds of chemotherapy. This treatment, the oncologist had hoped, would prevent the tumor from growing larger. Although it was not expected that the tumor would shrink or that the treatment would cure him of the cancer, it was probable that at the very least, it would allow him some time to get his affairs in order. In addition to the chemotherapy, my father also wanted to continue with the Aiijii Healing sessions.

The definite diagnosis not only brought a sense of urgency for me but for my father, too. Dad was never a touchy feely kind of guy, but he suddenly began to very freely reach out for hugs. "I feel like I can't get enough of them", he said, "I know that *love* is eternal, but the physical touch is something that I can't take with me," he clarified with his arms open wide calling for a hug.

As we embraced, I did my best to assure him that no matter how rough things might get, we would not leave him to deal with it alone. "We will all be here for you, dad, physically, emotionally and spiritually." Just as tears were about to drizzle down our cheeks, my father abruptly and skillfully changed the subject, thus, immediately corking our tear ducts. He had had enough emotion for the day. A few minutes of emotion were all he could take.

While some people who are looking death in the face decide to aggressively live life to the fullest and tackle a bucket list while they can, my father was more interested in spending time with family and enjoying every minute that he had with us. He particularly made it a point to let each of us know that we were loved by him. Dad had never been one to express his love in words but began to routinely say "I love you" during my visits and phone calls. I vividly remember the first time it happened. As I was getting ready to leave that night, he put his arms around me and squeezed gently. Then he slowly pulled away, not a lot, but just enough for him to see my face, his arms still looped around my back. "I know I haven't said the words enough over the years", he said apologetically, "but I just need you to know that I love you". As he paused to inhale a deep cleansing breath, his voice grew from a soft whisper to a strong, open and authentic tone. "I love you very, very much."

As I drove home that night, I excitedly called my sister-in-law on speakerphone. I wanted to share with her the wonderful gift that I had just received. Sharon, who knew my father well, and that he didn't often outwardly express his emotions verbally, was as moved as I was. As I went over every detail with her, we both sobbed as tears of joy drizzled down our faces. Our sniffles kept us from saying more. Although I had known that my father loved me, hearing the words from him was a beautiful song I will never forget.

MIDDAY

Chapter Eight

*"We must embrace pain and burn
it as fuel for our journey."*
~Kenji Miyazawa

With the emotional shock of his diagnosis wearing off and a treatment plan in place, Dad began to think about getting his affairs in order and to start tackling the "business" of dying, even though he was still hopeful for some additional time. At that point, he felt that in the event he makes a miraculous recovery, he would still be ahead in the game. But regardless of what was to come, the opportunity to use left brain logic necessary for taking care of business would be a welcomed relief from the emotional turmoil that had bombarded him the previous months.

By the grace of God, and still not in any physical pain, dad accepted and adjusted to "a new normal" with the start of a plan in place. It would be December before the chemo therapy would begin.

Our family spent many long hours in the attorney's office working out financial planning and caregiving options for mom in the event that dad were to leave this world first. Although Mom had already had a few close calls with death, it was clear that if she were to survive him, she would be unable to live alone.

Every day, my father grappled with the uncertainties about what might become of his wife of fifty-three years. He knew that she didn't want to go a nursing home, although she was already a good candidate for that kind of help. To talk about options and to get answers to our questions, our family spoke with a health care consultant about available choices open to us. We wanted to get the legal ducks in order to prepare for whatever might be in store for our mother. We were advised that if we didn't make decisions ahead of time, it would significantly reduce the options open to her if a change were to suddenly become necessary. After long thought, family discussions and Mom's approval, Dad was finally comforted in knowing that we would do whatever it took to keep her in their home for as long as possible with the help of a live-in caregiver.

In the coming weeks, with that task behind him, Dad was able to open short conversations with me about his dying. "Ideally", he said, "when the moment of death comes, I would like to have the family here with me. Not the entire family—just you, Donna, Bob and your mother. And to be clear, I want you all in the house, but not hovering over me". And that was that—short and sweet.

As a hospice volunteer, I was accustomed to quietly sitting by the bedside of my clients, often saying nothing, just being present with them and holding the space until the last breath. This is what I hoped to do with my dad. In my hospice training I was taught "*infinity breathing*" (a technique developed by Dannion Brinkley, co-founder of the "The Twilight Brigade"). "*Infinity breathing*" is a method of breathing together with another person in a way that is not only very soothing but creates a bonding experience for the people involved. To begin, I would match my breathing with my clients, inhaling when they inhaled and exhaling when they exhaled. When I found their rhythm, I would stagger my breathing so that when they started to breathe out, I would start to breathe in, thus making a kind of figure eight with each set of breaths, hence the name "infinity breath". It was always a very comforting experience for both my clients and me, and because they would simply continue breathing normally, they were not consciously aware that there was any particular method that was being used. Breathing had become the holiest of activities. When the end finally would come, the very last breath was especially a sacred moment. Sometimes I was blessed to inhale a client's last breath. I had hoped that by God's grace, my dad and I would eventually share the final moment like that, too. But as my mind revisited his wishes for his dying day, I knew that this might be considered "hovering". So I made an effort to reject that thought by soothing myself with "I'll just play it by ear and do what seems right at the time", thereby opening a possibility of doing it *my* way.

And so this was the second time I considered breaking hospice rules, which state that the patient should be allowed to leave this world in his or her own way and the caregivers must resist the temptation to make the dying time to be about them.

When the chemotherapy began in December, I offered to join Dad at the hospital to give him moral support while he received his treatments. I was glad when he agreed because it seemed like a nice opportunity to help develop the kind of father - daughter relationship with him that I yearned for. I really couldn't remember as a kid, doing any kind of specific activity with him, just me and my dad, without my siblings in tow. In the early days, he worked a lot and in his spare time on Saturdays he helped his father in his painting business. Unfortunately, family time was often sacrificed. So I was happy to have a chance for special time with him. And it's not that going to the hospital together was the perfect date, but at least we would be sharing the time together, so I looked forward to it.

But when the first day of chemo arrived, and I arrived at his house, Dad chose to follow in the "Kish tradition" of facing challenges independently. He also felt that it was more important that I stayed with Mom in his absence since her condition was more serious than his was at that time. He decided it was best that she not be left alone because she had been falling more than usual lately. He assured me that he was still feeling relatively okay and able to navigate the treatment process without help. Being a little disappointed about changing my plans for the day, I unenthusiastically followed his directives. I also realized that I had almost inadvertently begun to make his cancer diagnosis to be about *me*; that is, cater to *my* emotions and *my needs* to bond with my father in my way, and perhaps to even gain some control of his journey. This, of course, was totally unacceptable, and I knew it. He was the captain of his ship and it would stay that way for as long as he was able; even though logically I was well aware of that my own emotional needs were still silently screaming to be heard. Luckily I recognized that I must contend with those needs in a way that would not take my father's power away from him, particularly at a time when he would be dealing with a series of his own losses.

When someone is diagnosed with a terminal illness, the grieving process begins at that very moment, not only for the person facing death but, as I discovered, for all loved ones involved.

Elisabeth Kübler-Ross, M.D. a Swiss-born psychiatrist, and author of the groundbreaking book "*On Death and Dying*", identified five stages of grief and mourning that are experienced by people from all walks of life who are faced with a loss of any kind, particularly a loss related to death. These five stages of grief comprise of denial, anger, depression, bargaining and acceptance. They are described as follows:

Denial is a psychological defense mechanism that allows a person to initially "not accept" a reality or fact pertaining to a painful event, thought or feeling. By denying painful facts, it allows us to keep moving to tend to necessary tasks without stopping to face the painful emotions and demands of reality. This defense mechanism, however, will not work long term. Denial is a perfectly natural first response that can be temporarily helpful until the mind is ready to deal with the shock of a crisis.

Anger can manifest in different ways and is usually brought about by experiencing a loss of control of oneself, another person or a situation. The anger may be directed at inanimate objects, complete strangers, friends or family or even oneself. For those dealing with their own terminal illness or the illness of a loved one, the anger may be directed at God, or at those who are not suffering an illness or can even be directed toward caregivers who are unable to help them to get better. Logically, although we know we shouldn't be blaming others, doing so can ultimately result in feelings of guilt, which also must be dealt with.

It is also not unusual for loved ones or caregivers to become resentful of the one who is ill for causing them emotional pain or for leaving them. The cycle of anger, resentment and guilt can be exhausting for anyone going through it.

When the ***depression*** stage sets in, feelings of despair and hopelessness can affect a person's thoughts, behavior, and feelings so much that life can seem unbearable. Some people might feel that there is no point in even bothering with anything because their suffering is just too great. But no matter how difficult it is to feel such sadness, regret, fear, and uncertainty, there is a positive side to depression. Depression can also be categorized as "preparatory grieving" or "anticipated grieving" and can be seen as a kind of acceptance that carries emotional attachment with it. This shows that the person has at least begun to accept the reality of the situation that he is in, even if not completely. And fortunately, depression can be treated.

Bargaining is a desire to try and gain back some control and to make things right. Traditionally the bargaining stage for people facing death can involve attempting to bargain with God, usually by asking for more time with the promise to live a better life or become more religious.

Acceptance. Is when one can recognize and acknowledge the reality of the truth and can say and believe, "It's going to be OK.". It is a time when a person can allow himself to refocus his hope. In a broad sense, acceptance is an indication that there is some amount of emotional detachment and objectivity involved. It's not unusual for people who are dying to enter this stage a long time before the people they are leaving behind.

These five stages of loss and grief don't necessarily happen in any particular order or for any specific length of time. As a matter of fact, it is not uncommon for the patient and his family members to bounce back and forth between each of these stages or even to experience more than one stage at the same time, such as being both depressed and angry. To complicate matters, each individual can be, and most likely will be, in a stage different than the other family members at any given time. This alone makes supporting one another difficult and a prime time for unresolved family dynamics to erupt. Each individual has their own way of dealing with grief so judging one another for having different feelings, reactions and responses would be especially undeserved. It is helpful to remember that the grieving time is not a time for criticizing each other, but for empathizing with each other.

For both patients and their loved ones, negative feelings such as anger, sadness, anxiety, guilt and fear will most likely be expressed at one time or another. The emotional shock from facing the threat of terminal illness can be overwhelming. All of these emotions are real, and they need to be identified, acknowledged, and expressed. Having patience with oneself and others will go a long way toward the healing process. Every phase into the unchartered territory of a terminal illness brings many unfamiliar and possibly sudden changes that call for the continual acceptance of another "new normal". For people who have difficulty dealing with change under normal circumstances, this can be particularly difficult.

Chapter Nine

"Even the smallest changes in our daily routine can create incredible ripple effects that expand our vision of what is possible."
~ Charles F. Glassman

Since dad was craving physical contact, I got the idea of giving him foot and hand massages. It wasn't something I was used to engaging in, but I decided that it would be beneficial to him since both hand and foot massages are known to relieve stress and anxiety. Even though I wasn't familiar with the specific techniques used, I knew that the Chinese and ancient Egyptians have been utilizing pressure points of the hands and feet for thousands of years to promote health and well-being. And I knew that in today's world it is a valuable part of complementary and alternative medicine.

Up until that point, the thought of actually touching someone's feet had always creeped me out. I didn't even like to touch my own feet! We certainly were not a family with pretty feet, and quite frankly, most of us had feet that were downright ugly. However, by the grace of God and lucky for me in this circumstance, Dad's feet definitely fell in the normal range of the spectrum. So I came to the conclusion that if a foot massage would help my father, I would take a chance and go outside of my comfort zone and touch them. In addition to my resolve, his enthusiasm for this new activity also gave me the boost of encouragement that I needed to follow through on my great idea.

I decided that a foot massage, rather than hand, was actually a good place to start because feet, being situated on the ends of long limbs kept me at enough of a distance from him where I wouldn't be viewed as "hovering" for any length of time. Much to my surprise, putting my hands on his feet wasn't as bad as I thought it would be. I began to enjoy it almost as much as my father did! He very quickly began to look forward to this relaxing time together and so a ten minute foot massage was added to our schedule on the days I was visiting.

As anxieties grew for everyone, it wasn't long before the hand massage was added to our repertoire of comforting activities. The difference between the two was that the foot massage was done in silence, the hand massage, being closer to his face, was more friendly and social. We talked, laughed and reminisced. With his hands nestled in mine, I could not help but think of the many things those hands had done over the years…my father's hands had carved all of the holiday turkeys and Sunday roasts back in the days when a formal mid-afternoon roast beef dinner was the routine after returning from church. Speaking of church, I remembered my father's strong hands lifting me onto the merry-go-round at the annual church carnivals, the part about church that I enjoyed the most. My father laughed as he recalled that every year a few days before the carnival, Donna and I would ride our tricycles down the hill at the corner of the street and miscalculate the turn in the sidewalk, causing us to fall from our bikes and bang up our faces and knees. Not that it was funny, but because it was like clockwork that we went to the event every year covered in scabs.

When I was about four years old, I remember my dad's hands offering support as my baby brother was taking his first steps… and I'm sure he held his hands out to me too, when I became a walker, even though I don't recall it. As the memory came up for my father too, his eyes pooled. "Tell your brother that I want to meet with him privately," he said almost weeping with desperation in his voice. "I don't think I ever told him that I loved him".

After giving him a moment, I continued scanning the bookmarks of my mind, and saw his hands re-attaching training wheels on the little red bicycle that was handed down to me when Donna grew enough for a bigger bike. I remember the excitement as I watched and waited for his hands to finish tightening the bolts. Then I hopped on the bike and rode behind my sister like a big kid!

In my mind's eye I saw my father's hands moving checkers across the checkerboard and jumping over my red playing pieces as he crowned his kings. But there were times when he let me win! Sometimes we would play "Go Fish". When his hands shuffled cards I was mesmerized as the two halves of the deck gently flapped together. It was more fun for me to watch him shuffle than to actually play the game! We laughed as we recalled how he ended each game session with "Fifty-two Pick-up". He would arch the deck and make the cards fly high into the air for me to pick up afterward!

I could even see his hands as he demonstrated how to throw a football with a spin-- actually he was teaching Bob how to do it but I happened to be there, and so I joined in on learning the technique. Even though I never pursued the sport, the skill came back to me when my first child was born. It dawned on me that if I tucked the baby under my arm like a football, I would have my other arm free to do daily chores.

Every hand massage session brought more memories, not all happy ones, but cathartic just the same, in this stressful and difficult time of our lives.

"At what point did you stop suffering from the eating disorder?" my father asked one day during one of our sessions. In a previous conversation on the subject, brief as it was, I had mentioned that there are clear parallels between eating disorders and addictions. I suspected that his real question was asking if I was still controlled by it. I was happy to tell him that I had become completely one hundred per cent cured of the bulimia, but it was not without doing the hard work of learning to love, honor and respect myself. The process of building my self-esteem, confidence and self-acceptance took years. "Ironically, when I became pregnant with Rashid", I assured him, "I no longer felt a compulsion to binge and purge". Maybe it was a biochemical change that occurred during the pregnancy but I also believe that that there was also a spiritual connection taking place. In considering the symbolic and reciprocal language of Spirit, of which I had become very familiar, when I gave my baby the gift of life, his presence in my womb, in turn, gave *me* life. And it was a healthier life than I had ever had before! I have not ever been able to think of any of my pregnancies without the memory of when I briefly met death in the midst of my personal storm. And I intuitively understood that I needed to become a mother, especially after I heard that a lactating mother has the power to both nourish and comfort her child and this is the power of physical life itself!

With the start of my father's chemotherapy, the "treatment phase" quickly accentuated the "being ill phase", bringing new challenges and symptoms that were both emotional and physical. It is common for the side effects from medications, even more so than the illness itself, to change a patient's life so much that negative feelings just come tumbling out. This is what happened with my dad. He was feeling quite well until the treatment got underway. He was about two or three weeks into treatment when the uncomfortable physical side effects set in, such as fatigue, mouth sores, nausea, diarrhea, and constipation. Sadly these side effects were accompanied by severe pain that he had dreaded so much, although not from the disease itself but a result of the treatment. He also began suffering from memory lapses and confusion. Eating became unpalatable and toileting became torturous. "I made a big mistake", my father wailed with his dark brown eyes wide in shear panic. "What have I done to myself?"

A growing and tormenting anger began taking root within him from believing that he had made things worse by opting for chemotherapy. "You have a right to change your mind and stop the treatment" I reminded him. He openly admitted that it seemed as if the entire "healing project" had gone awry, but at the same time he was also afraid to stop the treatment. He still held a thread of hope that it would buy him some more time, perhaps until a cure was found or at the very least, to handle the rest of his affairs. At the hospital, he had become friendly with other patients also suffering from pancreatic cancer. Some had been on chemo for years and still had a satisfactory quality of life. The possibility that he could be one of them was enticing. Should he make an attempt to stick it out?

This had become one of his biggest struggles. As an engineer his entire adult life, my father typically was guided by probabilities, and now his decisions were reduced to possibilities. To make matters worse, he was losing trust in himself. His anxiety soon went through the roof, and as a result he would pace back and forth for hours on end. He also added a ritual of removing the shoes he was wearing and replacing them with different shoes, repeating the act over and over again, as if changing his shoes would give him a different path to walk. But this didn't give him any comfort or solace. Confused and terrified, he placed his hands on my shoulders and blurted out "I just don't know what to do!" "Let's just dance" I suggested, and so I wrapped my arms around his neck and we danced. I don't really know what made me say that, as there was no music, but somehow we both imagined that there was.

In a sudden flashback, I was about six years old standing on my daddy's feet as he did the two-step, first with me, then with my two siblings. The only other time I remembered dancing with him was at my parents' twenty-fifth anniversary party. I was a little bit drunk, I recall, and I think he was just trying to hold me up. Had I chosen to have a typical wedding, we might have danced on my wedding day, but my husband and I decided to have a simple civil ceremony at the house with only family members attending; just twelve of us in all. There was no music or dancing, but we did have great food and the traditional "to die for" Kish desserts. As I reminisced in my mind, I had no idea what Dad was thinking, but apparently the imaginary song ended because we both stopped dancing at the same time. Without saying a word, Dad found his way to his recliner and settled into it, closed his eyes and went to sleep. When he awakened, he seemed to have made a decision about his treatment plan. "Do you think I might get better?"

he asked. "I'd really like that but maybe we should just see what happens", I answered.

My father had never been one to give up on anything and this was not to be the first time. He would stick out the last few weeks of the first round of chemotherapy and decide the next step when the time came. He bravely stepped back onto the emotional rollercoaster.

Each day brought more anxiety. Every time he wanted to be productive, to do something around the house or call his golf buddies, he just wasn't feeling up to par. Believing he was losing control of his life, depression set in. It quickly developed into anger and guilt for not having the strength to "pull out of it", as he put it.

It was getting increasingly difficult for him to care for mom. Over the past few years Dad had made himself responsible for organizing her medications into daily pillboxes for morning, afternoon and night to easily administer to his wife at the appropriate times. This amounted to her ingesting almost forty pills per day. And now he had his own prescribed list, most of which was meant to reduce some of the side effects of the chemotherapy. The kitchen counter resembled a small pharmacy.

Dad had always been meticulous when it came to weights, measures and math. But now he was finding it hard to concentrate. He had begun to get obsessed with keeping track of time, asking every ten minutes what time it was. He would stop and stare at the calendar for long periods each time he walked by it.

Even though he had marked all of his important appointments on the appropriate days, he complained that he didn't understand how the weeks were set up and if the appointments were correctly posted. He deduced that "the calendar was all mixed up". After observing him, I figured out that he was getting the numbers on the calendar confused with the digital clock with its numbers constantly changing by the minute. He admitted to having a hard time remembering things and expressed his fear that he would give mom the wrong pills or give her the correct pills in the wrong amounts.

Between my siblings and me, one of us was there to help during the day on most days, but the nights when we were gone brought more challenges for our father. Apparently he wasn't getting much sleep because as soon as he got settled in, mom would be getting up. She had always been a night owl, but was more so now since her medication guaranteed that she would sleep the day away. Every night as the clock struck midnight, as if preprogrammed, she would wander through the house all night long until her feet would get tangled in her walker. My mother, even when healthy, was always pretty good at falling, whether on roller skates, ice skates, a horse, climbing a mountain, walking or dancing, so much so, that it had become a private family joke. Now that she was unable to get up by herself, it was not so funny. The muscle relaxants that were prescribed for her markedly increased the risks for falls. After a particularly difficult night, Dad was in tears the next day as he described what had happened the night before. He heard his wife crashing to the floor. He got himself out of bed as fast as he could, placed his hands tightly on the handles of his walker and made his way down the hall to rescue her, only to get his own walker tangled in hers as he bent down to help. Then he fell on top of her, unable to move. The two of them were wedged in a small space between the kitchen counter and the refrigerator, with their jumbled up walkers pressing against their frail bodies. Feelings of helplessness had overpowered my father's insatiable desire to always fix things. It was almost two hours before they managed to free themselves and return to bed.

After hearing his heart wrenching account, my brother declared a call for action. In an emergency meeting with my sister and me, a plan was quickly put in place. We hired a nurse to come by weekly to assess mom for any changes in her condition. She was also to keep track of medications, call in refills for prescriptions and to sort pills for the week for both Mom and Dad. My sister-in-law would cook extra for dinner and deliver it to their house every evening since she and my brother lived only a few minutes away. We would all take turns staying the nights. I also ordered a special clock that I found online that was created specifically for the elderly struggling with confusion or dementia. It featured a clear, analogical display of the time, included the day of the week written alphabetically, as well as an alphabetical month and numerical date that was designed to be easily comprehensible. I concluded that my father had become so concerned with the calendar and clock because he was painfully aware that his days on this earth were numbered. He needed a way to keep track of time and try to gain some stability with an ordered schedule that he would create for himself.

In the days following the walker debacle, Dad began opening conversations with me about God. He had friends who were deeply religious, and even though he respected their beliefs, he never thought that formal religion was for him. He admitted that he felt a conflict about what he was taught about religion and what he believed was true for him. He made the choice to stick to pondering only his spiritual beliefs and leaving religion out of it. "God is here no matter what", he said, even though he didn't share with me his own definition of God. And I didn't ask him either. Perhaps that was still part of the journey on which he still needed to embark. I trusted that he would find answers in his own time. With that, Dad fell deep in thought and no words were exchanged between us.

As the afternoon turned to dusk, my father confessed that he was feeling a bit guilty for actively and consciously thinking about God now only because he was ill. "I don't think that I ever really included God in my daily life when I was well. Do you think there will be any ramifications for that? , he asked. "I sincerely doubt it", I said. "I don't think God is a punishing God." But no matter what, I, for one, can vouch for him that he did often include God in his life, in that he often said "Thank God Almighty…." on many occasions for whatever the situation called for. Perhaps that was just an unconscious habit but in my eyes, thanking God is thanking God, no matter how you look at it. He also expressed that he has never had any desire to make any deals with God, as one of his friends often did, and he didn't think he would do so now.

Soon he was drifting off again to a world deep within himself, his eyes open and staring but fixed on nothing in particular except what lay in the interior of his mind. Finally he broke the silence. "Gerry was telling me how his daily prayers had developed into bargaining sessions with God. He would promise to do better in his life, change his bad habits or just do more good deeds if only his loved ones could be healed. But I think you're right", he said. "I don't believe that God has been punishing Gerry, I think he was just feeling guilty about something and was searching for a way out of his guilt. We all have our own ways of being religious or spiritual", he concluded.

"I've made plenty of mistakes in my life but most I don't regret because I learned something from them" he continued. "And the others I'm still working on", he admitted, and then returned to his contemplative space far away.

.I suspect that my father began revisiting every mistake that he had ever made. I soon discovered that he was also concerned about any mistake he might make in the future.

It wasn't long before his mind rejoined me in the room. He began apologizing in advance in the event that he should say something mean or hurtful to any of us while in a drugged state. He brought up his last conversation with his mother as she lay dying in a hospital bed. He was shocked beyond belief as she suddenly began blurting out horrible accusations, saying things that were far out of character for her to say and simply just untrue. He loved her so much and the thought of losing her was bad enough without the harsh words that hurt him so deeply. The pain had been unbearable as he was thrust into a pool of intense and crippling emotions – the kind he normally avoided by stuffing them away. But this time, he wasn't sure he could save himself from drowning in such pain.

Luckily, after he spoke with his mother's medical staff, my father came to the conclusion that these episodes were directly related to the drugs she was taking which left her with no control of her words. But just the same, he was still extremely hurt and distressed by the experience.

Knowing that he may very well be in a position to be ingesting mind altering medications as his illness progressed, he worried about unintentionally inflicting the same kind of pain on the people he loved. So it was essential for him to apologize in advance to let us know not to take such an occurrence to heart, should it happen. Dad wanted even more so to let us all know how much we were loved and cherished by him and so he continued to tell us often and the bear hugs increased.

The day finally arrived when Dad announced that his driving days were over. "I feel that my reactions, response times and spatial judgements are lacking" he told me matter-of-factly. "I hate what these drugs are doing to my brain. It just burns me up how I need to take them and wish I didn't have to, while there are people who actually *want* to feel this way and would do anything to get their hands on these poisons....I just can't understand how the hell anyone would want to feel this lousy…but to each his own…", he added, trying not to judge.. Then he handed me his car keys, "Let's go to the liquor store to get some alcohol-free wine for your mother." Mom had always enjoyed her wine with dinner, but since she had been taking prescribed medications, she had resorted to drinking the non-alcoholic type. Dad was always thinking about others and despite his own problems, he kept a mental note of when the non-alcoholic wine bottles were getting low.

As we made our way out to the car, I noticed some new scrapes and dents on the bumper, but kept my observations to myself. I was grateful that my father realized and accepted that this life change was necessary and that he didn't try to resist it or slip into denial of the new limitation. "Thank you, God", was all I needed to say.

Chapter Ten

"Write your hurts in the sand. Carve your blessings in stone."
~ Anonymous

AFTER THE FIRST round of chemo, we had learned that the tumor had decreased in size by seventeen per cent! This was a huge surprise to the oncologist who didn't expect any shrinkage at all, and so encouraged Dad to continue to do whatever he had been doing. Although we will never know for sure, we had attributed the shrinkage to the strictly scheduled Aiijii healing treatments, and mom was the first to say that she believed that to be the case.

This certainly was good news, so good, in fact, that it was enough for Dad to make the decision to trek on with the chemotherapy for a second round while also continuing with the Aiijii healing sessions. To a certain degree, his body had adjusted to some of the more troubling side effects from the treatment which made it less agonizing for him to continue. Additionally, he still wasn't experiencing pain from the tumor, as it hadn't grown to press on the peripheral nerves that were entwined with it. He didn't actually have "good" days, he described his days as "bad" and "not-so-bad". This was an improvement from before. Despite his constant fatigue, Dad made it a point to walk as much as possible from one end of the house to the other. He strongly believed that a body in motion will stay in motion. When he was sitting, I would often catch him doing leg lifts. He didn't want his muscles to atrophy. My father was determined to not give up, "I still have some life left in me", he would say, "and a few more things to do".

As spring rolled around, Mom's condition worsened and we made a decision to hire a home health aide during the week. We wanted her to specifically focus most of her attention on our mother. She would also keep one eye on Dad who had fixed his mind on being as independent as possible for as long as possible. This worked out well because Mom needed much more attention than she had been getting from us. She had always been a social butterfly and quite enjoyed being the center of attention when the situation allowed. She particularly enjoyed meeting new people. Even in her prescription-drug induced state, her eyes lit up when she met Florence, a very kind and friendly woman from Ghana who showered her with love and attention. Florence invented ways to stimulate Mom's brain and distract her from the excruciating pain that she lived with. They laughed together often. My father was pleased.

This worked out well for me too, because I was able to take Dad to his chemo treatments without worrying about Mom falling or getting herself in a jam while trying to do something that she was no longer capable of doing. A few weeks earlier, Donna had caught her climbing up a step ladder to reach something that she didn't need on the top cupboard shelf. Our mother's determination had always been both an admirable asset and a curse, but particularly now it was the latter, now that it was interfering with her safety.

When I entered the hospital parking garage Dad didn't mind if I had to park far from the hospital entrance. He welcomed the walk for the exercise that it gave him. Once in the hospital, he introduced me to his friends in the chemo room; the friendly nurses with positive outlooks and the other patients who cherished every breath they took. I was touched by the camaraderie and upbeat attitudes of everyone there. Some came alone; others had a doting loved one at their side. Dad made it clear to me straight out, that I was not to cater to him. He had his routine and was able to do things for himself, at least for the time being. And anyway, I was his "guest". The socialization of the treatment process was good for him, as it allowed him to take a break from thinking and worrying. He even fetched snacks and drinks from the snack bar for those who were less mobile. Dad was always a good host. He was happy and at ease making sure others were comfortable. The only difference now was that he dragged the IV apparatus with him.

Dad's lifelong motto was to do the right thing and *always* follow the rules. In the fifty years I had known him, I only saw him break a rule once--and that was during his chemo treatment at the hospital. In the corner of the treatment room there stood an ice cream station. Attached to it was huge sign that read "For patients only!" About an hour into treatment Dad whispered with a wink "Psssst, hey Karin, do you want some ice cream?" "I'd love some but it's against the rules. The sign says it's only for patients", I responded. With a huge smile he said "rules, schmules" and then stood up and shuffled over to the freezer, dragging his IV with him. He returned with two vanilla ice cream cups. And together we ate our ice cream as if we were on a date in an ice cream parlor. From that time on, Donna saw to it that the freezer at our parents' house was always packed with containers of Edie's Ice cream in almost every flavor. It had become the go-to comfort food for all of us.

As time went on, it seemed that Dad continued to get thinner by the minute. My siblings and I continued taking turns staying overnight, and sometimes my daughter or my youngest son took over. Hassan was always good with old people, and even though he was just seventeen, he was already a certified nurse's assistant. This accomplishment was almost accidental. He hadn't been very diligent in school and needed all the credits he could get to finish the school year. It turned out that his school offered a summer program that was meant to keep kids out of trouble and give them some life skills. The two courses offered were Hospitality and Certified Nurse's Assistant (CNA). The attractive thing for the kids about the program was that the city would pay them a small salary to take the course and pass it. With a little money as the motivator, Hassan was all for it. He was already familiar with nursing homes because when he was younger, I had often taken him along with me when I visited the residents. And he truly enjoyed it. Now he had an opportunity to help his grandpa who was happy to have special time with him, too.

When the weekend arrived for his first time "on duty", I had a feeling that it might bring some memorable and perhaps defining moments in my son's life. My hunch proved to be correct. His father dropped him off at my parents' house just in time for him to assist his grandfather in the shower. I guessed that he hadn't shown up entirely prepared emotionally for what would transpire in the bathroom that day. It was years later when he finally was able to express and share his thoughts and feelings surrounding the experience. In Hassan's own written words, he recalled that day as vividly as if it had just happened.

"I always saw Grandpa as a role model. And he was a man who was exactly that; a good man, successful, motivated, loving, strong and approachable. This is how my grandfather presented himself to me; this is what I saw, and this is who he was.

And then the unbelievable happened. The power of reality showed its formidable face right before my eyes! It was totally shocking! The man was literally deteriorating in front of me! And just as I saw it, he saw it also, the stark reality hitting him for the very first time. I stood staring at him as he stared at himself in the mirror. There was a moment of disbelief on both our parts. We were feeling the same thing at the same time except that he was my elder; a leader, a real man in the presence of a young man, a boy, lost and confused in life and even more so at that very moment. He seemed to sense how our thoughts melded together as we both stared at the man in the mirror.

My Grandpa is just skin and bones, I thought to myself, still in disbelief. "Look what this cancer did to me, do you see this?" he said motioning to his ribcage with hanging, wrinkled skin draping over his old bones. As we continued staring at the mirror, his body seemed to be disintegrating right before our eyes! How the hell is this possible? How can this happen to exactly the kind of man I'm supposed to become? Then he dropped the towel from his waist as he prepared to step into the shower. I was glad I was there to assist. There was so much confusion racing through my head. But suddenly I realized that he was still the man he always was when I caught a glimpse of the confidence that seemed to be emanating from him. I saw a man who dealt with the cards that he got dealt. He slowly stepped into the shower and as the water hit his body, he became relaxed. His eyes closed. I held my hand behind his back for support. With his lids still shut tight he explained, "Sometimes in life things don't turn out the way you expect and you just have to deal with it. You do what you have to do." He paused as the water splashed over his face. Then opening his eyes he said just two words -- "Finish school." He was still the same man I admired and loved, despite his unrecognizable, skinny and sickly shell of a body. He was a grandfather with his grandson who I don't think ever thought he would need assistance taking a shower."

Three more rounds of chemo left Dad extremely weak and sick. He seemed to have forgotten that he still could make the choice to discontinue the treatment due to the fact that his oncologist consistently encouraged him to trek on with it. Many doctors are typically torn between suggesting a new phase of hope with hospice care and continuing with aggressive treatments. Statistically, terminally ill patients enter into a hospice care program in the last two weeks of their lives, causing them to miss out on just about all of the benefits that hospice has to offer them and their families. Perhaps because a physician's goal is to physically heal, they perceive hospice care as a personal failure.

Once a month during the chemo treatments, my father and I would touch base with his oncologist, who would answer any questions or address any concerns we might have had. On one particularly difficult day, Dad asked how long he would have to continue with the chemo. Without even thinking, his doctor blurted out "Until you die". I was shocked. My father sat flabbergasted and shaken as the knife twisted in his heart and killed his hope. "Let's get out of here", I said helping him from his chair. "We won't be coming back."

The next day, I made an appointment with another physician who, I had hoped, would be up-front and honest with my father about his illness and also have a good bedside manner. I was looking for someone who would discuss any options that might be open to him, including entering into a hospice program. Although I had previously mentioned a hospice alternative, I suspected my father wanted to hear it from a doctor.

The new physician was young, compassionate and down to earth. I could tell that Dad was comfortable with him. Together they determined that the most humane thing to do in this particular situation would be to discontinue aggressive treatment. My father seemed relieved in some ways, because it allowed him to begin to accept a new phase of hope; a phase where his priorities would change to focus on being comfortable rather than on being cured. But even as hope took on a new direction, my dying father understood that many losses would be woven into it.

He would continue seeing the doctor every two weeks solely for the purpose getting weighed and to stay informed of his current medical reality. The doctor reminded him that if or when the day came that he no longer wanted to know, that he could by his own choice, simply stop going. Dad truly appreciated being given that power.

I, too, was both relieved and grateful when this young, compassionate oncologist paved the way for, and was in complete favor of my dad entering into a hospice program. It wasn't long before my father decided that the time was right to move into this level of care. He had asked lots of questions about the benefits of the program and liked what it had to offer. I chose to call Vitas Hospice, an organization that my Connecticut chapter of The Twilight Brigade often partnered with. As the Vitas staff members -- the doctors, nurses, CNA's, chaplain, and social worker began to come to my parents' house, I was thrilled and honored to learn that the social worker assigned to my father's case was one who had participated in one of my *Twilight Brigade* trainings a year before! It was a rewarding feeling for me to see how my volunteer work came full circle!

Chapter Eleven

*"Carve your name on hearts, not tombstones.
A legacy is etched into the minds of others
and the stories they share about you."*
~ Shannon Alder

Dad enjoyed developing new relationships with the hospice staff. Even though they were there to cater to his illness, he used the opportunity to regain some contact with the outside world by asking about their families and their interests. Ironically, this wonderful team brought some life back into the house. It was a welcomed change for us all after focusing completely on caregiving and dealing with feelings and emotions that were being pushed, pulled, and tossed around from every angle. We learned that one of the aids was a mother of twins, another had a teenage son who auditioned for American idol and made the first few cuts! Another spoke of her childhood years in Africa. As time went on, there were several CNA's, four nurses, a chaplain and a social worker coming to the house to help my father. He began to keep track of their schedules and looked forward to each and every visit. Every one of them gave him something to smile about. They all loved him because he was kind and gentle and he always made it a point to remember everyone's name.

As the chemicals from the chemo therapy gradually left my father's system, his body responded positively by giving him some strength to continue taking care of the necessary business affairs of dying. The hospice intake questionnaire that he had previously filled out had requested information about final arrangements. He had purposely left that portion blank for a future time when he thought he might feel ready to think about it. And that time had come.

My dad had always been certain that he wanted his body cremated, following the footsteps of his parents and predeceased brother; but at that point, he was unsure what he wanted us to do with the cremains. He was also unsure if he wanted a wake prior to the cremation. As we gathered around the dining room table that night, we entertained several options such as burying the urn in the cemetery near his parents and brother, or sprinkling him into the wind at a location meaningful to him, or taking the cremains on a boat ride into long island sound to be gently swallowed by the ocean waves. What started out as a theoretical, peaceful and humorous chat unexpectedly turned into a full blown cat fight between our parents! Mom vehemently rejected the cemetery idea. Although she wanted to be near her husband when it was her time to go, she had no interest in a final resting place with his father! Insulted and hurt, but willing to compromise and please, Dad considered other cemetery options, such as being laid to rest in a different cemetery altogether, amidst flowering shrubs, chirping birds and quiet neighbors. But Mom wanted no part of that either. The cremains of her sister had been set free from a hot air balloon above Denver, Colorado. In comparison to that dramatic departure, the thought of a cemetery was far too confining in her view. My father added that he liked the idea of having a headstone that bore his name as well as having a place for survivors to visit, should they choose to do so. As the brainstorming and discussion on the subject came to a close, it left him exhausted and rattled emotionally, but paved the way for more serious contemplation.

During this time period, at Dad's insistence, we all gathered for a visit to the funeral home to make the final arrangements. Always thinking about others, he wanted to get this task out of the way so we wouldn't have to worry about it later. Although he knew he was getting closer to his dying day, it was still somewhat of an abstract thought since he was still able to walk around, albeit with some difficulty, and still able to make sensible decisions which was validated by his reaction and response to the previous squabble on the subject a few nights before.

At the funeral home we met with the director and completed the required forms. We then eerily followed her to the downstairs level of the building where the casket showroom was housed. It was filled with both very elaborate styles of burial boxes as well as a few simple designs. There were also urns of all kinds, shapes and sizes—from mason jars, to mahogany, silver or golden containers made in all types of geometric and heart shapes, porcelain angels, ducks and cars, as well as wind chimes and bird houses. And for the environmentally conscious, there were biodegradable floral and animal themed containers meant for ocean burials. My mother, sister, brother and I stood quietly and somberly as Mom's husband and our father slowly examined each display. Even though it was creepy to witness, we allowed him as much space as possible for his thoughts and feelings.

Gradually, his facial expressions hardened as irritation began to build within him. "Holy Mother of God!" he exclaimed. "Look at this body! This is not me! This body is just like old worn-out clothes that are so exhausted that they could not even be passed down to another user! Look at these damned prices on these things! I'm not going to display this old outfit in an expensive display case so people can gawk at me and whisper about how much money we did or didn't spend!" He made the decision at that moment to bypass the wake and opt for a quick cremation immediately after death. Then he added," I don't care if you put this old piece of rag in a cardboard vacuum cleaner box for the cremation, just as long as I don't have to waste money on some beautiful case that will just be burned! I would much rather spend the money on a big party for all my friends and family to enjoy. And make it in a nice restaurant with an open bar after the memorial service!" Looking at each of us he added, "Do you all understand?" We all nodded in unison. And so that was settled.

CHAPTER TWELVE

"Funerals...are for the living."
~ John Green

DO YOU HAVE any ideas about the kind of memorial service you would like, Dad?" I asked. "I can help you to plan it so we can finish filling out the Hospice form." That's a good idea," he responded, "The nurse had been asking me about it. Let's get it out of the way." I had never planned a funeral before but I had participated in a funeral planning workshop several years earlier. I had learned that in planning this type of event there were several elements that when combined together would make a meaningful service meant to honor the deceased and begin the healing process for the mourners. The workshop stressed the importance of encouraging the mourners to express a myriad of emotions, and then ultimately leave them in a positive and joyful state of mind. Dad and I casually discussed music, readings, and prayers. "Nothing too religious or too sappy" he instructed me, and as a United States veteran he added. "And I don't care how you do it but I want someone to play "taps" and present your mom with the American flag…. and don't forget *Amazing Grace* at the end". I made a list of each of his requests and also noted where he would allow me my creativity. That night I began the task of putting the service together. I started with a quote and a paragraph about the circle of life. The tone was solemn but hopeful, which I felt created an ambiance worthy of the respect and dignity my father deserved. Proud of my good start, I continued on. But the next sentence unexpectedly stopped me in my tracks, *"During this sacred time we wish to honor Donald Emery Kish with the highest appreciation we can send him."* I wrote. And then suddenly, seemingly out of nowhere, I broke down. As tears streamed from my eyes and plopped onto my keyboard, I quickly deleted his name from my screen and replaced it with a "fill in the blank" line. I could not bear to see my father's name in a document speaking of the deceased. I would get back to finish writing the opening words at another time.

Still traumatized, I made the decision to add a candle lighting ceremony as a meaningful healing tool to signify that the spirit and memories of the deceased would continue to live on and burn brightly. I spent the next two hours composing a poem and tracking down an instrumental version of "I Believe I can Fly" to pull it all together.

The next component would be a short biography and eulogy that I would read at the service, followed by an invitation to others to share their special memories. According to my workshop notes, this part of the service is often the most meaningful and remembered element as mourners affirm the significance of the life of the deceased. As those in attendance pass through contrasting emotions of laughter and tears, the healing process begins.

Taps and the presentation of the flag came after, followed by the Lord's Prayer, a beautiful musical rendition of "Alleluia', and then finally, to complete the service, a vocal of "Amazing Grace" that would be sung acapella by a family friend.

The next day, I presented my draft to my father containing all but his name and the eulogy for his consideration. Without saying a word he sunk deep into his black leather recliner chair and slowly read through the document. When he reached the end, he returned to the front page and carefully read through it again. He repeated the process several more times showing no expression. Finally, he raised his head, looked into my eyes and nodded. "I like it", he whispered handing me the manuscript, "I don't need to see this again".

CHAPTER THIRTEEN

"The wound is the place where the Light enters you."
~ Rumi

THE TIME WAS now ripe for another round of depression, but this time it would be to an even deeper level than before. To my father, the days seemed torturous and never ending. He longed to get up and about and do something productive but his weakened body stopped him. He longed to sleep peacefully but his busy mind stopped him. His fears had taken control of his once logical and practical thinking. "Who's the captain of this ship?" he wailed. He knew he was gradually losing control of the helm.

I don't know what she said or what methods she used but one of the hospice nurses whose name was also Donna, (and deemed as my father's favorite) was instrumental in pulling him out of this cycle of depression. It was not uncommon to see him hurriedly scuffling to the front door in his big, red, over stuffed cartoon-like slippers that I had given him for Christmas at least ten years before. Whenever he heard the sound of her car pulling up he would open the door wide and call out her name; "Doooooonnnna! Dooooonna! Hurry! Hurry! His sigh of relief when she walked into the house was heartening. Perhaps it was her upfront but kind ways of communication, or deep understanding of the monsters he faced, but whatever it was, he was always reassured and comforted by her.

Another source of light that came into his life during that phase of depression was a sweet, cute, young CNA from West Africa. Her name was Fadike but he referred to her as "Angel Cake". It was obvious that her soft spoken ways, warm smile and sincere interest in hearing what he had to say tugged at his heart. He normally didn't talk about his growing up but while she sat beside him glued to his every word, he led her through his childhood and young adulthood while sharing with her his favorite activities and happiest times in life. It seemed as if reminiscing about happy times had rekindled a glimmer of gratitude and hope within him that had recently laid hiding behind his dark eyes. After Angel Cake's shifts were over, he would often sit quietly for hours, not sleeping, but silently reflecting, it appeared, and perhaps contemplating about how those happy memories of his past might influence his present struggle.

Chapter Fourteen

"It's OKAY to be scared. Being scared means you're about to do something really, really brave."
~ Mandy Hale

Not completely out of the emotional woods yet, the coming week brought more restlessness and anxiety for my father, which was made worse by the fact that he was unable to stand up by himself. He was always a pacer even when healthy, which often drove us nuts over the years. The fact that he constantly needed me by his side to help him to stand and then sit down every four or five minutes brought him even more angst. Although he was glad I was there for him, he let me know that he hated putting me through that. "Not a problem", I would respond every time, especially since when he managed a standing position, we danced as I held him up. It was only for a few short moments but at least it was enough to relax him some and it put him in a different frame of mind before he needed to sit again. His two-step was perfect. The long sliding rhythm of his feet kept perfect timing with the imaginary music that we became accustomed to listening to. And he seemed to enjoy it. "I'll bet you've never danced so much in one day", I remarked. "I never knew you even liked dancing!" "I've always liked to dance;" he replied, "just not with your mother!", he added with a smile. Mom always insisted on leading. Dad needed, more so now than ever, to be in control.

He described feelings of being hurried along by life when he didn't feel ready for what was to come. It was "like being a piece of luggage that is dragged through an airport without even knowing where the plane will land", he shared.

Terminal restlessness is a syndrome that is often observed in patients at the end of life. It is considered a hospice crisis and meets the criteria for starting a continuous nursing level of care because it can include introducing new medications that need to be monitored. After a hospice team meeting around our dining room table, changes in the treatment plan were adopted. Nursing care began around the clock, in part to give my siblings and me, who had been staying there full time by that point, a breather and much needed rest from the constant caregiving that had become our daily norm. We were pleased that our father's anxiety level and restlessness subsided some; however, it wasn't long before unanticipated reactions brought changes to his demeanor.

The physical touch that was comforting to him just a few days before had unexpectedly become unpleasant. In addition, due to either the new meds or the illness itself, Dad's thinking processes began to slow and as a result, normal levels of activity going on around him suddenly felt invasive and overwhelming to him. "I'm feeling trapped" he would say, especially when someone was leaning over him for routine caregiving or for hugs. Even my mother's good intentioned hand holding made him feel uncomfortable and imprisoned. I had learned in my hospice training that when holding a patients hand, it is good practice for the caregivers hand to always be positioned underneath the patient's hand so if he should decide to pull away, he can do it easily and remain in control.

Aside from those unexpected side effects, within a week, Dad's body seemed to adjust to the new drugs. His mood improved considerably; he was good-humored and noticeably calmer, but this was not to last long. After ingesting a few more scheduled doses of the newly prescribed cocktail, Dad began to experience random, unfocused, haphazard hallucinations. He was seeing ice cream dripping from the ceiling and the room seemed to be spinning wildly. "I think I'm going crazy!" his terrified voice called out. During one of the worst episodes, in a sudden blink of the eye my father fell into an unresponsive, catatonic state of consciousness. The certified nurse assistant, a kind young man who was just starting his career, was scheduled for the over-night hours. He had been cleaning my father up for bed when it happened. He tried talking to him gently in a reassuring voice but could not get Dad to snap out of the stupor he was in. My father just sat limply on the small stool in the bathroom, his head facing downward and his arms dangling at the sides of his bony ribcage. The young CNA did not know what was normal for my dad, as the Kish family was a new assignment for him. So he called for my help with the matter. This situation was new to me also and I too, was not sure what to do in this case, but like him, I chose to try and encourage our patient to respond. I tried to keep my tone calm and tender, hoping my father would gradually come out of his trance. Then, as I spoke again, his eyes suddenly opened wide, the whites like golf balls, the irises a dull, dehydrated shade of brown. My father sat staring at me as if trying to figure out who I was and why I was there. "It's Karin", I responded, "let's get you to bed, you look tired". "Are you going to help me?" he asked. My dad's clearly articulated words came as a surprise to the hospice worker who hadn't yet heard him speak. "This guy won't help me", my father complained. "I kept telling him that I am tired and want to go to bed, but he just stood there looking at me". I glanced at the young man who kindheartedly just shrugged. We both knew that this conversation had taken place only in my father's unconscious mind.

As I walked him to his room, I hooked my arm into his to keep him steady. He made me promise that I would help him. He went on to explain that he had been seeing things that made no sense to him, things that scared him and made him feel uncomfortable. Although astute enough to realize that the hallucinations he was experiencing were caused by the drugs, he was still somewhat confused. I think those Hospice people are trying to kill me!" he declared, catching me off guard. "Please!" he begged, "do not let them kill me with those drugs! I have rights! Remember? You told me I have the right to be involved in my own treatment! Remember? REMEMBER?? Promise me you will not give me those drugs! Stay on my team!" In his last ditch effort to make sure I understood him, he placed his hands firmly on my shoulders. While steadying himself, his dehydrated brown eyes stared deeply into mine until they latched onto my soul. Promise me, PROMISE ME, HONEY! Can I trust you?" "Yes, you can trust me. I promise you Dad, no more of the new drugs. We both need to sleep now." As he sunk into his bed for the night, I administered an Aiijii Healing and he finally drifted off into a restful sleep.

The next dose of the cocktail wasn't scheduled till morning. With the hospice nurse due to arrive that same day, I decided that I would first talk to my siblings about our father's concerns and decision and we would work this out with the hospice team when the nurse arrived. One thing I knew for sure, and that was that I was on his side. I totally agreed with his decision. The roller coaster ride that he was on had led him right back to the anxiety that the pharmaceutical "cocktail" was expected to help. I was sure we would all agree that the side effects were far worse than the anxiety itself. And I was convinced there was a better way to help him.

The next morning, Dad awakened bright and early. This particular day he wanted to make sure he was alert and clear-minded for the CNA's shift change because that is the time when the meds were to be administered.

Emotionally exhausted from the night before, I slept a little later than usual that morning. When I woke up, it was to the sound of commotion coming from the kitchen. Apparently, it was time for Dad to take his pills and he was refusing them. I could hear Donna and the night aid trying to convince him that his medication would make him feel better, but he would not hear any of it. "You're all trying to kill me!" he cried, and then announced that he was going to call the police. With that, I jumped from the bed and ran to the kitchen. From my position, I had the easiest access to the phone, an older style landline with a long spiraled wire attached to the receiver which my father had stretched around the corner into the living room. He had already dialed 911 and was about to tell the dispatcher that his family was trying to kill him. I quickly placed my finger on the cradle button and disconnected the call. "You lied!" my father shouted at me with tears in his eyes, "I thought I could trust you! I thought you were on my team!"

Just then the phone rang. It was the police dispatcher inquiring about the "emergency" since the call did indeed go through, but was disconnected. I explained that my father was battling cancer and was having adverse side effects from some of the newly prescribed drugs, and as a result he became convinced that we were trying to kill him. I went on to say that I had promised him the night before that we could revise the treatment plan but I hadn't yet had an opportunity to talk to my other family members and his health care providers. I assured the dispatcher that everything was okay and that I was confident that we could get the situation under control. I promised to call back if we needed their help.

After hearing my explanation, my father had calmed down. It saddened me that his feelings of desperation were so deep that he had resorted to calling the police. I could not imagine the sense of betrayal he must have been feeling. As I replayed the incident in my mind, my father was busy opening the daily pillbox and pouring its contents onto the counter. By this time, the morning CNA was in the house and ready for her shift. As the neutral party, and with no knowledge of the previous events, Dad had chosen her to disclose to him one by one, the name of each pill and its usage. He had agreed to take the drugs he had normally taken before, while refusing those that made up the new cocktail.

Later in the day, we met with the hospice team who were officially in agreement to abide by the wishes of their patient. This also re-established our father's trust in both his family members and the extended caregivers, which went a long way in reducing his anxiety level.

With the cocktail eliminated and that ordeal behind us, we all breathed a sigh of relief. However, Dad still had another concern. He became worried that if his restlessness returned, it might infringe upon his wife's sleep since they shared a bed together. He also feared feeling isolated in the bedroom, knowing that the day would come when he reached the stage of immobility. As an engineer, Dad always analyzed every situation fully. Earlier in his illness we had previously talked about the possibility of having a hospital bed delivered to the house if or when the situation warranted it. I immediately determined that the time was now right and so made a quick phone call and the bed was brought in within two hours! The delivery team placed it in a spot in the living room where due to the layout of the house, my father could not only have his privacy but the ability to view and/or easily take part in the other goings on in the household. And mom could get her rest as her schedule permitted.

Chapter Fifteen

*"What you have perishes; what you are
survives beyond time and space."*
~ Unknown Author

As my father's physical condition worsened, friends and extended family members began calling and asking if they could stop by for a visit. For some who hadn't seen him in a while, it was a shocking experience because his body had deteriorated so much. There was one particular get-together with extended family that proved to be healing for everyone.

As always, Donna prepared a typical tasty dinner. An effort was made to keep the conversation happy and uplifting. Laughter slowly but surely made its way around the dinner table putting everyone at ease. It wasn't loud laughter, but a soft, all-embracing, peaceful kind. Dad wasn't eating so he remained in his hospital bed in the living room where he had a good view of the dining room table and the people he dearly loved seated around it. I thought it ironic that he watched us from a distance. In a conversation just a few days before, he had expressed his wishes for us to continue living our lives to the fullest after his passing. He wanted us to be happy and to hold on to good memories.

After dinner, we all gradually made our way back into the living room where dad had taken up residence. I had previously shared with my Aunt Ann about my father's sudden yearning for physical touch, even though I had never known him to be a "touchy feely" kind of guy, and how our daily hand massages helped to fill that need. She was already aware of the relaxing benefits of a hand massage and stress reducing qualities that it can bring because she, too, enjoyed regularly scheduled visits with her masseuse. She suggested that we all take a partner and take turns massaging each other's hands. Her suggestion was at first met with reluctance and strange looks, since most of my family members also were not the touchy feely type, but surprisingly everyone began to take part. The intimacy of the moment proved to be soothing and restorative for everyone. A loving energy permeated throughout the room. Then a beautiful thing happened. My father began expressing his appreciation to each individual, one by one. He realized that this may well be the last time he saw many of them and he wanted his good-byes to be meaningful. Sincere words of gratitude and love flowed effortlessly from his lips until he could say no more. Needless to say, there was not a dry eye in the house, including Dad's. After a long and sob filled silence, my father could take no more. "That's enough of this sissy stuff", he abruptly declared, "My mascara is running". We all burst into laughter.

Chapter Sixteen

"Now we know that if the earthly tent we live in is dismantled, we have a building from God, an eternal house in heaven, not built by human hands."
~ Corinthians 5.1

WITH MEDICATION-RELATED HALLUCINATIONS eliminated, Dad could at least get back to contemplating the life that he had lived and noting where he needed to tie up loose ends in relationships or otherwise. As it turned out, he apparently began to receive help from above which brought not exactly hallucinations as such, but a type of visions that would be new to him; the kind of visions that I believe are better described as "apparitions". Rather than causing anxiety or fear, these visions typically prove to be meaningful and helpful because they provoke deep, meditative thought for the person experiencing them.

These episodes ultimately allowed my father to successfully begin to evaluate different phases of his life which, in the end, allowed him to enter into a place of peace within himself.

According to Ineke Koedam, a seasoned hospice caregiver, counselor, researcher and author ("*In the Light After Death*") it is not uncommon for dying people, in the days or weeks before death, to talk about visits from deceased loved ones. "They say that these individuals have come to collect them, or to help them to let go of life," she explains, pointing out that many people are reluctant to talk about such experiences because they are afraid of being seen as confused and then required to take medication they don't want. Also, some of the hospice staff avoids talking about theses visions as they do not want to appear unprofessional. Relatives often shy away from discussing such things for fear of ridicule. Luckily for my dad, because of my own experiences, I was actually waiting for it!

One of the first indications that Dad was on the brink of entering another realm of consciousness and interacting with inhabitants that the rest of us could not see, initially came through a vivid dream which occurred shortly after the problematic pharma-cocktail left his system.

For at least a week, my father was mostly quiet as he sunk into his black leather recliner, bundled up in cozy fleece pajamas and of course, his big, red, pillowy, cartoon-like slippers.

By Wednesday, he finally spoke aloud and announced that he was in the mood for a party. Although he had seen some extended family members just two weeks before, he had not yet seen his grown grandchildren who were living out of state or away at college. So our task that week was to gather them all together for a typical Kish bash even though we were mindful that it might be somewhat awkward for the kids who had limited or no experience in witnessing the physical effects of terminal illness. We were all well aware that they would be seeing a different grandpa now that the cancer had ravaged his now frail body.

Upon my father's request, I was instantly reminded of the previous discussion concerning his funeral when he had made it crystal clear that he didn't want his passing to be a sad occasion, but rather, similar to any other Kish event with good food and drink with a celebratory flavor, so that was the kind of atmosphere we were aiming at for this event. My siblings and I sensed that this party would mark an especially important day in our father's life.

Saturday arrived quickly, and as planned, the menu had been completed and the shopping was done, and Donna proceeded to produce her usual magic in the kitchen. The day nurse, with one eye on dad, sat and observed us as we all scurried around getting ready for the six grandkids to arrive from the airport or long road trips. Luckily the weather was behaving nicely; it certainly was not typical of a northeastern winter. Normally late November / early December brought snow and bitter cold, but this year we had been blessed with balmy conditions boasting temperatures in the mid to upper 60's.

By midafternoon, the kids started arriving one by one with updates on their college lives and activities. Although Dad was quiet, he appeared especially happy that everyone was able to make the trip to see him. Everybody, as usual, gravitated around the dining room table; however, my father chose to stay resting in his hospital bed situated in the center of the living room and watch from afar. I knew he was tired, probably even exhausted, although his face showed signs of content, but I was still somewhat surprised that he didn't join us at the table for more direct interaction with his grandchildren, who, after all, were the reason he called this gathering in the first place. I planted myself at the table in the seat that was closest to the living room where I could keep an eye on my father in the event that he needed some kind of assistance. The day nurse, of course, was also available.

As dinner was served, much to our surprise, Dad managed to pull himself up into his walker with no assistance from any of us. Suddenly, all conversation stopped and all eyes turned to him as he began making his way towards the dining room. The sound of the tennis balls that had been transformed into feet at the bottom of the legs of the walker slowly and steadily hit the floor with a soft, methodic clunk; clunk and then scuff, scuff, clunk, scuff, scuff, as his cartoon-like, overstuffed, pillowy red slippers moved him forward. When he reached the table the walker came to a halt. Then he made a deliberate forty-five degree turn to face his family. "I'm really glad you all came", he pronounced in a stoic and stately manner. "If you don't mind, I would like to go to sleep now. Enjoy your meal and have a good time. Thank you all for coming." It seemed so odd to me, almost like he had energetically disconnected himself from us. He hadn't even had a chance to intermingle. Then he proceeded to his bedroom. I followed behind him, as did the nurse.

When we arrived at the bedroom door, he turned to the hospice caregiver and suggested that she return to the dining room. "I won't need you here right now", he said kindly. "You can go help my family". With that, and a bit stunned, her chin spontaneously tucked under, her eyebrows raised and her lips pierced while her eyes shot me a confused but obeying glance. Then she promptly left the room.

I want to sleep in my "real" bed one last time, he explained. Can you help me take off my slippers? Sure, I responded, as I untied the shoe lace on the silly sneaker-shaped overstuffed red slippers. Then I pulled down the covers and tucked my father neatly inside. "How about one of those healing treatments?" he suggested, "I want to make sure I am really relaxed for this". Odd thing to say, I thought, he is only about to take a nap.

Just as I was arranging the pillows, my daughter, my father's only granddaughter, finally arrived at the house. She had gotten a late start that day from the university. She cautiously entered the room to see her grandpa. As she drew closer to his bedside tears welled up in her eyes. "Don't cry honey", he responded. "This old body may be falling apart but the love I have for you will last forever. It will never leave, don't worry, everything will be okay. Go eat some dinner and have a good time. I hope you don't mind but I need to sleep now. I love you". Saida gave him a hug and left the room trying desperately to hold back her tears.

As the bedroom door closed behind her, I held my outstretched arms to the heavens, and silently asked God that I be used as a conduit for healing energy. I could gradually feel a Divine force coming into my energy space as I entered into a deep meditative state. The healing Guides (heavenly helpers) proceeded to do their thing to create a healing environment, by the grace of the Almighty God.

When the healing session was complete, my father was in a deep, sound sleep. My re-entry back to normal awareness swiftly followed. I quietly left the room, leaving my father alone and returned to my spot at the dining table.

Dad was asleep for at least two hours when a night nurse, whom we hadn't met previously, arrived for the shift change. After being introduced to everyone, I offered to give her a tour of the house so she would know where everything was. Glancing at the empty hospital bed in the living room, she appeared confused, ".Where is the patient?" she asked hesitantly, "has he already passed? Am I too late?" "No, No! I assured her, he's asleep in his room. Come! I will show you," as I led the way down the hallway. As I quietly opened the door and tiptoed inside as to not awaken my father, I was surprised at what happened next. "Mr. Kish, Mr. Kish!" she enthusiastically called out loudly. "How are you this evenin'?"

Startled, my father apparently was awakened abruptly from the dream-state. And clearly, he was extremely confused. "Who is *she*?" he asked, motioning toward the unfamiliar woman standing in his bedroom doorway. "This is the night nurse who will be here to help you tonight. I was showing her the house and brought her in here to see you". Still trying to get his holdings on waking reality and totally out of character for him, he blurted out angrily, "This isn't the time and place to meet new people! As I caught the nurse's glance, I could tell that she was feeling a bit uncomfortable. Without saying a word, she slowly turned around and left the room returning to the other family members in the dining room.

Meanwhile, still confused by his surroundings, my father questioned me in a quiet voice "Am I dead?" "No", I replied, assuming he would be happy to hear that. But much to my surprise, he became increasingly upset after I told him that death hadn't come to him yet. He definitely was not happy with this news. His dry eyes would have been in tears had he not been so dehydrated. Shear panic was quickly etched onto his face. "I was the next person in line", he wailed. "I had been waiting there for hours and because of *her*. (the new nurse) I need to start all over again! It was such a long line and I was next! The very next person!" he reiterated. Then, without hesitation, his eyes began roaming the room taking in every detail and distracting him momentarily from his despair. After a short reprise, his eyes turned to me. Heeeyyyy, where did all those people go?" "You mean the family?" I asked confusedly. "They are in the dining room". "No, no!

I'm not talking about the *real* people; I'm talking about the *helpers!*" Although I needed more information to completely understand what he was saying, there was no need for me to ask any questions because my father went on to explain. There were "lots of people-like helpers" around, busily engaging in various activities. It looked to me like they were taking down a circus tent or something. Everyone had a job to do and they all worked together like they knew the routine." Then he added, "You know that hospital bed in the living room? They took the whole thing apart--completely disassembled it and moved it out!"

As he returned back to his panicked state my father cried, "So what am I going to do now! I was next in line and everything was ready! Now I need to go back to the beginning! What am I going to do?" he ruminated over and over again. I was at a loss for words and didn't know how to resolve the problem and make him feel better. All I knew was that my father believed that he needed to get to the front of the line and that the journey had been long and hard. The thought of having to start all over again was clearly causing him distress.

Meanwhile, the rest of the family was in the dining room eating cake and catching up with each other. It was a rare event that we were all at the same place at the same time. After much turmoil of trying to come to terms with the fact that he wasn't dead and contemplating about what to do, Dad concluded that the only thing he could do was to go to the family and explain what had happened. He was always a firm believer in family meetings -- he liked things out in the open with no secrets and with everyone on the same page.

This particular meeting would prove to be a difficult thing for him because I quickly came to realize that somewhere in his mind, my father believed that everyone in the house also thought he had died, and that they had already accepted that fact. He thought they would be shocked and disappointed to learn that he was not actually dead! He had known that his illness had been an emotional rollercoaster for everybody and he didn't want this news to send everyone back on the dreadful ride, especially when he believed the healing process had already begun for everyone. I tried to explain that nobody thought he had already died, they were all waiting for him to awaken from his nap, but he didn't believe me. His dream had been so vivid he was certain it was real.

"Wait for me while I collect my thoughts and figure this thing out," he said. Dad sat wordlessly while I sat on the other side of the bed and waited. He was determined to handle this his way and based on his look of resolve, I would not deny him that. I waited awhile longer in silent patience as my father struggled to find the words to explain to the family that he had been knocked out of line and would have to begin his journey again. Finally, after a silence that seemed like it would never end, my father looked up from his thoughts. Using a serious and powerful tone he announced "Okay, it's settled. Can you help me put my slippers on and get me out of this bed and into the walker? Then I'll be able to walk without your help to the dining room."

I followed behind him as his determination slowly guided him down the hall to where everyone was sitting. I felt relieved that his walker was cooperating with him so he could arrive safely for his speech. But no sooner had I completed my thought, the walker came to an abrupt halt. My father caught a glimpse of the hospital bed in the living room. This changed everything that he had planned to say! "Wait a minute! That's the bed that they took apart, and now its back! All the helpers will have to do all that work all over again!" Once more he was confused, upset and frustrated, and once again, all conversation stood still, silence filled the room and all eyes were on Dad. Looks of concern stamped the faces of everyone seated around the table. They all turned to me for an explanation of his odd outburst. As I carefully described what had happened, it soon became clear to everyone in the room that what this man needed was words of encouragement. My first born, the oldest of his grandsons, quickly took the cue without a hitch, and lovingly opened his heart to speak. "I am so proud to have you as my grandpa", he began. "I'm so glad I made the trip from North Carolina to see you because we still have so much to talk about. Do you remember the time when……?

One by one each family member expressed to our father, grandfather, husband, brother-in-law, and father-in-law how much we loved him and how happy we were that he was still on this earth. As the room swelled with love, encouragement, pride, affection, deep appreciation and gratitude, the last person to contribute was the new night nurse. Her wise, honest and eloquent remarks tied a bow around the personal gifts of love that we presented to the frail looking man standing before us that evening. "When people are terminally ill," she began, "they think a lot about how and when their life will end. When you know it will be happening, it's not unusual for the imagination to visualize the ideal death. But God plays a role in that picture, too. And God is the only one who knows when your time is up and it seems that your time just isn't up yet. When that time comes we will all do our best to make it as comfortable and easy as possible for you. In the meantime we will do our best to make your *living* as comfortable as possible." As we all took in her words, it felt as if the depths of our souls had melded together as one love.

In my mind, I recalled the feelings that I had when my consciousness abruptly re-entered to my body again after my brush with physical death. It initially felt like a setback to me after experiencing the freedom of being out of my body. My father's disappointment and reaction to his vivid dream was so similar. He was so close to the anticipated freedom of leaving his diseased body behind when he thought he was the next in line....

I believe that this incident was the beginning of the acceptance stage of my father's dying process and opened the door to the next phase in which he longer had a fear of death.

Inter-dimensional travel is not limited only to physical death. It can also occur at any time even *before* the end of physical life as long as the energetic body is vibrating at such a frequency as to partially disengage from its physical counterpart. This is a natural occurrence and happens routinely during sleep and dreamtime and while in various altered states of consciousness, such as during meditation when the unfocused mind sets the energetic body and consciousness free.

As we dream, we are often whisked off to a land of symbolism — the secret language of Spirit. Dreams can offer clues that can help us to resolve matters in our current waking lives. Dream interpretation is a very useful tool that can bring the workings of other planes of reality into our awareness. Through our dreams, we may also come in contact with deceased friends or family members or even catch a glimpse of an event that hasn't happened yet.

That same week, I too, had a special dream. When I awakened from it, I recalled every detail. In the dream I looked out the back door of my parents' house and there, sitting on a bench, as if at a bus stop, was my deceased uncle (my father's brother), a baby, and two other men I couldn't identify. Although they said nothing, I knew in the lucid dream that they were waiting for my father to join them. I woke up shortly after, feeling a sense of peace.

Later that day, when my brother arrived, I privately shared my dream with him before updating him on the day's events. Unlike me, he didn't think anything of it, that is, until the following night after getting Dad ready for bed. We had the same routine every evening which consisted of giving him a sponge bath, brushing his teeth, administering (non-hallucinogenic) meds, dressing him in fresh bed clothes and then tucking him into the hospital bed. That particular night, no sooner had we completed the process and tucked him in, our father frantically began pulling at the covers "I need to get up!" he exclaimed, adamant that we help him to his feet immediately. He had experienced an uncontrollable need to pace. So, back and forth he walked; to the front door and then back to the couch, and then repeated the trek numerous times again. Dad's big, red, over stuffed cartoon-like slippers knew his pacing routine well. But this night after about the third or fourth round, the slippers came to a stop, our father slowly raised his shaky hand and pointed his index finger at the easy chair in the corner of the room, a chair that looked empty to my brother and me. Then he deliberately turned his head in our direction and asked "Whose baby is that sitting there?"

This validated for me that my dream was much more than just a dream. This incident marked the beginning of my father's death bed visions. I, of course, was thrilled, my brother, a pragmatic engineer, was flabbergasted and wasn't quite sure what to make of it. To my knowledge, he probably hadn't ever thought of these things before, and even if he had, I don't think it was something he would categorize as "real".

TWILIGHT

Chapter Seventeen

"I've had faith my whole life that there was someone looking out for me, a spirit guide, a soul guide."
~ Lady Gaga

IT WASN'T LONG before the second vision took place. My father had become a lot less anxious, especially during the daytime hours, and began spending more time sitting in his wheelchair which allowed him the ability to either relax or to move about as he wished without much help from others, that is, after he was initially seated into it. It was not that he wheeled himself around a lot but his red cartoon slippers were given an opportunity to work less tirelessly than they did when he stood up and walked using the walker. The wheelchair made it easier for him to move about while those silly slippers peddled the floor and became an engine, transforming it into a Flintstone-like vehicle of transportation. This gave my father at least a smidgeon of control over his mobility when losing control was one of his biggest challenges. Mostly he sat quietly and contentedly staring into space once he parked himself in the corner of the living room near the open door. The full glass storm door appeared to protect his daydreams from outside weather conditions, which, in that particular year, was mostly rain. I don't know whether his intention was just to look out at the neighborhood that he had lived in for fifty-three years or to uncover a brand new world through that glass; perhaps even, another plane of reality that may have been attempting to come into view. On this particular day, after sitting for almost two hours it seemed a kind of fusion was taking place between my father's divine mind and his human mind.

I say this because seemingly out of nowhere, in a clear and strong voice, Dad blurted out, "Do you know Eddie?" "Eddie who?" I asked. "Eddie Bauer" Dad responded matter-of-factly, as if I had been privy to his thoughts. Well that's a strange question, I thought; wondering where it had come from. I had never seen my father wearing the Eddie Bauer label or seeing anything in the house of that brand, for that matter. I guess I was taking too long trying to figure out why he asked that odd question and what had seemed to me to be at an even odder moment. "Well?" he impatiently prodded, "Do you know him or not?" "I don't actually know him but I do know that he is a clothing designer and that he has a clothing and sporting goods store in the mall." I offered. "No, no! I don't care about that", my dad said, with some frustration in his voice. "I just want to know what kind of guy he is; what kind of character he has. Why don't you go ask your mother; she might know." "Now, this is getting even more strange", I thought to myself. Mom was often heavily medicated due to her painful neuralgia, but miraculously, at that exact moment, she happened to be awake, up and about and amazingly in a pretty clear mind, so I popped the question at her which she didn't seem to think was strange at all. After reviewing her memory banks and sincerely trying to be helpful, my mother answered, "I don't ever remember meeting him, so I don't know anything about his personality, but I've walked by his store plenty of times -- never went inside, though. Too expensive!" she remarked, ending the conversation as she continued plucking her eyebrows with the limited vision she still had left. She had always preferred the sale days at the big box stores rather than designer labels. As my sister-in-law entered the house, she too was asked the question, and perplexedly, could offer no more information than her mother-in-law or me.

I wonder why he needs to know about Eddie Bauer's character, I said out loud to myself. Surprising me, my father blurted out "Can't you see him? I need to know because he is *here* and he wants me to follow him!" I initially thought Dad may have been a little confused and perhaps had been recalling a dream after sitting so long in silence. But silly me, my father knew precisely what he was talking about and went on to make it perfectly clear to me that he wasn't interested in following Eddie Bauer if he wasn't a good person. "I want to make sure he has good morals and believes in God, he continued. "I don't want to follow a schmuck." Resigning to the fact that the situation was a serious one to him, I took off my judgmental hat and offered to look online for information. The web, however, only chronicled Bauer's career path and company information, but not anything about the man's personality or moral character. Feeling the need to tell my father something that would answer his question, I assured him that Eddie Bauer is a nature lover and rationalized that he must be man who loves God. I don't know if he thought I was just appeasing him or if it my research satisfied his curiosity even if only a little bit, because he said nothing in response. The subject was dropped as suddenly as it had come up and was not mentioned again for the rest of the evening; however, it was not to be the end of it.

When the sun came up in the morning, the ringing of the phone brought unexpected news. On the other end was my oldest son, Rashid, calling from North Carolina to let me know that he was at the airport and on his way to the Eddie Bauer corporate headquarters in Belleview, Washington. He was employed as a distribution planner for another retailer and due to his success in that position, he had received an invitation to interview for a position at Eddie Bauer Corporate.

Upon hearing the news, I was completely blown away by the coincidence as thoughts raced through my head about whether or not I should tell him what had happened the night before. After swift consideration, I opted to play that part cool and casual but first, as a proud mom, I joined my first born in the excitement of this amazing opportunity that I felt he well deserved. "While you are there," I nonchalantly added, and assuming that Eddie Bauer was alive and well, "I hope you have an opportunity to actually meet the man to find out what kind of guy he is..." Before I could say more, my son interrupted me. "Mom, in the first place, Eddie Bauer has been dead for 20 years and what do you mean you were talking about the label yesterday?! That's random!" Feeling I had no choice, I began my next sentence with "I know this might sound weird, but this is what happened..." I went on to explain everything, and about how his grandpa had some concerns about Eddie Bauer without knowing more about him. When it was happening, I, too, thought the conversation that day was random, but looking back on it, especially after learning that Bauer was indeed in spirit, I have been able to see the bigger picture.

At the time, I didn't know how the interchange between the spirit of Eddie Bauer and my father initially came about, but one thing I knew for sure, is that the situation offered a dying man a choice when the ability to make choices were becoming more limited while also giving him some control at a time in his life when he was loosing control of just about all aspects of his existence. And so this was indeed a gift.

I also believe that my son's appointment for the interview was actually a "God orchestrated" tool that created an energetic path to draw Eddie Bauer to my father for the purpose of helping him. In the end, Dad received what he needed. In my eyes, this proved that Bauer was a spirit of good character and morals. About two weeks later out of curiosity, I had asked my father if Eddie had still been visiting him. He responded, "No, he's not here anymore because I made the choice not to follow him but he sure is a really good guy!" Incidentally, Rashid was offered the position at the corporate headquarters, but he turned it down. He decided that he would rather live in California. That same week he received another offer from another retail chain in San Francisco and was able to use the offer from Bauer Corporation as a bargaining tool, which in the end, helped land him the San Francisco job at a higher salary!

I have come to believe that every being, whether in the physical or spiritual form has a mission with the same underlying purpose: love, compassion and service to others. Throughout our existence we are faced with challenges that help us to reshape our soul, which in turn allows us to evolve spiritually. The fact that we all begin our existence as energetic beings and continue to be so even while encased in our physical form, allows the law of attraction to come into play and provide avenues for us to accomplish our personal missions as we are spiritually and energetically entwined with the people, the situations and the disembodied spirits who can help us.

Chapter Eighteen

"In truth, I have done nothing alone. God has called me and has been my pilot. The Holy Spirit has been my comforter, my guide, and my power source."
~ Reinhard Bonnke

For the next two days after Dad's encounter with Eddie Bauer, my sister and I were in disagreement regarding our father's treatment plan. She had a career as a psychiatric nurse for her entire adult life and was very familiar with hallucinations. Beginning with the DSM IV and now in the DSM V, (the Diagnostic and Statistical Manual for Mental Disorders) The American Psychiatric Association (APA) has categorized hallucinations in more depth than before and recognizes the differences between drug induced hallucinations, hallucinations caused from mental illness and spiritual visions. Donna was from the school of the DSM II, and rarely, if ever, had she encountered patients claiming spiritual visions. When our father's spiritual encounters began, she did not believe that they were helpful to him. She was more inclined to believe that he was too confused to make any decisions about his health care at this point in time. At the beginning of his illness, Dad had appointed Donna, Bob and me as his healthcare agents in the event that he could no longer make practical decisions. She believed that time had come.

Although he was no longer taking the previous drugs that caused hallucinations, he began to complain about side effects from the Clonipin that had been prescribed for anxiety. He had previously responded well to the medication but now his body's reactions to it had changed. Bob and I were the ones who carried out the evening medications routine and got our father tucked into bed each night, so we were also the ones who contended with the heartbreak of his protests regarding the Clonipin. Donna felt that he should take everything that was prescribed by the hospice team because they were the experts. Even though I trusted and supported the hospice team, I believed that Dad was still a good judge of what his body could tolerate. I could also see that he was struggling to maintain a certain amount of control over the situation. After previously having some horrible drug reactions he wasn't yet resigned to surrendering to every decision made by the rest of the team, although he did realize that there was some trial and error involved with each prescription, due to the fact each patient's body and situation was unique. This issue was really creating a lot of tension in the house between Donna and me. Following Dad's system of solving problems with family meetings, Donna had called a private meeting with Bob to get his take on the matter (of which I didn't know the outcome). Then she privately sat down with me, acknowledged my expertise in spiritual matters and then complimented me on the undivided attention that I had been giving our father by tending to all of his immediate needs. She was very sincere and I deeply appreciated that. She went on to say that as a nurse, she believed we should continue with the meds as prescribed because Dad was not in the proper mental state to decide these things for himself. After all, "he was having hallucinations", she explained. After hearing her out, I had to follow my gut feelings which happened to agree with our patient's feelings. In the end, I was still angry and upset with her and she was still angry and upset with me because we both would not budge even a fraction of an inch on the subject. Although Dad did not participate in these private discussions that we had, the air was so thick you would need a machete to cut through it. And so Dad called a brief meeting with his two daughters. His words were quick and direct; "Just work it out, he said, "because the last thing I want is to be the object of a family conflict." The following day, I don't know if my father planned it or if it just somehow happened, but he managed to take the matter into his own hands and seek an outside opinion.

Normally, after the hustle and bustle of the morning routine, dad would settle in for a nap, but on that particular day he decided to relax on the rose colored, swivel rocking chair that sat beside its twin with a small end table positioned between the two. I plopped myself on the matching chair and chose a magazine from a large selection of subscriptions that were always a staple at my parent's house for as far back as I could remember. Donna was out doing errands. It wasn't long before my father appeared to be in deep meditative thought.

Although I was focused on an interesting article, my attention suddenly turned to my father when I heard him say out loud in a calm, clear, and distinguished voice, "Yes, okay, Dr. Glock, I understand. To summarize what you just said, I can continue to take the Oxycontin, but it is of no benefit to me. The anxiety pill is good for me at night, even though the side effects are uncomfortable". His eyes were fixed on something I could not see. Then he paused a moment as if he were listening to someone talking to him and then added "Okay, Dr. Glock, thank you".

He then swiveled his chair in my direction and addressed me. Even though I had just overheard his previous conversation, he matter-of-factly explained to me that Dr. Glock suggested that he should take the Clonipin for anxiety at night because the benefits outweighed the side effects. He added that the doctor had informed him that although the OxyContin has not been benefitting him, it wasn't hurting him either. "I trust him", Dad said, "so it's settled. You and your sister will just have to accept that and stop squabbling". And then he said no more. Apparently, my father was able to get a second opinion about his medications from an invisible doctor who happened to come by to help. "I can't believe this is happening, I thought to myself, even though I had no doubt that it was entirely possible.

That night, even though we made no changes regarding the pills, Dad didn't complain when it was time to take them. Bob and I caught each other's glances and had our fingers crossed as we dispensed his medications, and then as our brainwaves intertwined, it seemed we read each other's thoughts "so far so good" we both silently reassured ourselves in unison, nodding to each other at the same time.

Because my father was unable to swallow larger pills, we had been giving him the OxyContin rectally, which wasn't pleasant for any of us, but it had to be done. Luckily, the other smaller pills would usually go down orally with a few sips of water or juice.

The next morning, I awakened early to dispense the regular morning doses since he hadn't complained the night before. When that was done, Dad asked to be seated on the commode that was positioned by his hospital bed for convenience. This had become part of the morning routine even though lately it produced little results, due to the fact that he hadn't eaten any food in almost three weeks. But this time was different. My concern on that day was that the suppositories would come out and another dose would be necessary. I was glad that Donna had offered to do it if needed. We left him his privacy on the commode as we waited nearby but out of site. My sister and I quietly chatted between ourselves.

When the painful sounds of gurgling innards had dissipated some and the malodorous backfiring stopped, we carefully removed our father from the commode. I quickly closed the lid without looking, dressed him up in fresh clothes and seated him gently on the couch. "A fine day for a new muffler", Donna remarked playfully, causing me to crack a smile. "Now to get that toilet cleaned", I thought to myself. Dreading the task, I slowly lifted the lid and was shocked at what I saw! It was as clean as could be with the exception of 38 fully formed OxyContin tablets lying at the bottom of the pot! Every pill that had been inserted in the last two and a half weeks had not been absorbed into Dads system! Dr. Glock was right, he could take the OxyContin pills, but they would be of no benefit! Even Donna could not argue the case for discontinuing those!

Dad had found a helpful friend in the "doctor in spirit" and had continued to converse with him daily. As a result, he appeared to be more relaxed and less anxious about his treatment plan.

CHAPTER NINETEEN

"You have to become the owner of the spiritual consciousness. You have to dwell in it. You have to have that smile on the inside of your awareness, and then you will radiate it out to all."
~ Unknown Author

AS THE HOURS ticked on, Mom had joined her husband in the living room on the couch, with Dad sitting beside her. "Hey Karin, come here!" He called out, gazing at me with a big skeleton smile; he had gotten so thin that his facial muscles had completely atrophied. I would not have even known he was smiling had it not been for the slightest glimmer of moisture in his dry, dehydrated eyes and the extra effort he took to make sure his mouth was opened in a position to show his teeth. "Do you see it?" he asked excitedly. Dad began describing other "rooms" that he defined as "superimposed over the physical room that we were in." He also spoke of the other beings in the room and he specifically wanted me to know that he understood the difference between the family members and the spiritual beings he saw because, he explained, those "other people" appeared less dense and less solid. "I know that your mother is physical", he assured me, as he gently touched her hand. And then pointing to the corner of the room near the fireplace he continued "and that cute little baby is in the other kind of room"….. Then after a moment he closed his eyes tightly and then quickly raised his eyelids while opening his eyes as wide as he could. He repeated this movement several times as if trying to prove to himself that he was truly awake, alive and well. Finally his eyes scanned the room slowly. "Where the heck is that kid's mother?" my father wondered out loud.

Then after a short pause and apparently still looking between heavenly planes and certain that he was indeed awake, alive and well, he wrapped it all up by saying, "You know what, honey? I think I am beginning to experience the mystery".

Chapter Twenty

"A lot of people resist transition and therefore never allow themselves to enjoy who they are. Embrace the change, no matter what it is; once you do, you can learn about the new world you're in and take advantage of it."
~ Nikki Giovanni

It was getting to the point where I couldn't wait to hear what mystical thing would happen next in my father's world. I think he, too, was amazed. I was feeling blessed that he was sharing his experiences with me, and as for my brother, he was beginning to get curious.

Dr. Anne Banas, a Hospice neurologist and palliative care physician, suggested that if, as care givers, we should encounter someone experiencing visions at the end of life, we need to ask

"Is there meaning to the vision?" "If there is meaning, does that need to be explored? Does it bring comfort or is it distressing? We have a responsibility to ask that next question. It can be cathartic, and patients often need to share. And if we don't ask, look what we may miss."

"Ohhhh! Ohhhh! Karin, do you see her? She is soooo beautiful!" "Who?" I asked. "The lady in the red dress", my father responded, still gasping at her beauty and teetering at the edge of glory. But then instantly, he seemed to forget I was there. He called out to her, "Please take my breath away! Please take my breath away! Please! Please!"

I would have liked more information, but I didn't get it this time as he slipped into what appeared to be a deep state of stillness, contemplation, reflection and possibly introspection, waiting to exhale, even perhaps permanently. It was hours before he opened his eyes. Whatever it was all about, he seemed to have come to terms with it. And for that, I was pleased.

Chapter Twenty-One

*"What you have perishes; what you are
survives beyond time and space. Death merely
marks the end of our physical aspect"*
~ Author unknown

THE NEXT EVENING after Bob arrived from work, our father had a special request of us. His legs had weakened considerably in the past days so he asked us to seat him in the wheelchair and take him through each room in the house, starting at the far end of the hallway to enter the bedroom that he had previously shared with his wife. "You two wait in the hallway while I have some time alone in this room", he requested. Having previously witnessed this sort of thing with other hospice patients, I had quietly explained to my brother that this was part of his letting go process. It wasn't long before our father announced "Ok, I am finished. This room looks good." He then directed us to take him to each and every room in the house while he made an assessment about the condition of each one. We quickly caught on that he wanted to leave each area in an orderly state.

I was reminded of the time when I was visiting a hospice client who I had guessed to be about a week away from death's door. She had asked me to tidy up her room and then to take her address book from the drawer and leave it on the nightstand by the lamp. When I completed those tasks, she requested that I bring the photos of her children and grandchildren that had been placed neatly in a row on the top of the dresser over to her so she could see them more easily. She explained that she wanted to spend time with each photo individually. As I handed her the first one of her oldest son, she cradled it in her arms and then closed her eyes for a moment. She then gently handed it back to me to return it to its spot on the dresser. She instructed me to place it facing the wall so she could no longer see it. "This is odd", I originally thought, but continued to do as she requested. We followed this process for all of her prized photos. Finally we came to the youngest grandchild. This one she held onto longer than the rest. After infusing it with her love and humming a lullaby, she motioned for me to take it from her. "Don't turn this one around" she said, "I want it to face me". When it was time for me to leave, this lovely woman proceeded to thank me for my visits and for my help, then gave me a warm hug and wished me well. "You can turn the baby around now," she whispered in my ear. On my way out, I complied with her wishes and then gently closed the door behind me. Two hours later, I received a call that she had passed away.

The conditions of each of the rooms in the house, thus far, were up to my father's standards. However, when we returned back to the living room Dad was horrified by what he saw. He proclaimed the room to be a disaster and without delay, and entirely out of character, he transformed into a drill sergeant! "Karin, Bob! Clean up this mess!" he commanded, "and do it as quickly as possible!" I have to admit that with all of the pillows, blankets, clothes, medical equipment, ointments, personal care items, medications and other medical supplies placed everywhere, he was right; the place did indeed look like a cyclone had hit. Exchanging glances with each other, my brother and I stood at attention. But before getting started, our father had one more request.

He wanted us to help him to his feet so that he could stand upright in the walker. Even though we had some concerns about his wobbliness, we followed his orders. We reasoned that it seemed a more appropriate position for him to be in to oversee what we were doing and give direction while having some control over the situation. As we cleaned and organized, Dad retreated between the scenes, speaking to and gesturing to others whom we could not see. He effortlessly switched his view back to our world when he needed to. "Everything looks much better", he said, praising us for job well done. "Now go get your mother, I want her here for the meeting". Donna was out walking the dogs, as she did every evening at that hour. Our father assured us that we didn't need to wait for her as her walks were generally long ones and the dogs needed their exercise. He promised us that he would update her after the meeting when they shared their special time together.

After Mom was brought in and seated comfortably, Dad scanned the room before taking rollcall of everyone assembled. He noted out loud both spiritual and physical beings alike, including the baby who sat alone in the corner chair without his mother. When he was satisfied with the attendance, he straightened his body as straight as he could stand and then in a very formal voice of authority he began. "I, Donald Emery Kish, hereby call this meeting to order to inform you all that the items in this room, other than the original furniture, will no longer be needed". Although we were accustomed to family meetings, Bob and I had never experienced this kind of performance from him. It was a sight to behold, our dying father standing so staid and confident with the air of a high-ranking official. We listened intently in anticipation of what he would say next when my brother and I both, at the same exact moment, landed our eyes on the big red comical pillow-like cartoon slippers that our father was standing in. The contrast in ambiance was more than humorous, it was downright hilarious. If nature had provided us with a specific hub in the brain or location elsewhere in our bodies to store unused laughter, it was about to burst at the seams. Our lungs had already involuntarily gulped in the comical air of our surroundings and so with no other way to hold it back; we exhaled, bringing with it an explosion of laughter. We tried desperately to conceal our hysterics by covering our mouths with our hands but there was no going back, for we had already passed the point of no return.

"Do you two find this amusing?" our father asked in a stern and humorless voice, totally unaware of the site that we saw in front of us. "No! no! There's nothing funny", Bob replied, finally able to contain his laughter and feeling guilty about the untimely outburst. "No, there's nothing funny", I added remorsefully when my father directly turned to me for my response. Finally, with our laughter in check, or so we thought, the meeting was back in session. Just as our father was about to continue, I made the mistake of glancing in my brother's direction and when our eyes met, our hands again simultaneously rushed to cover our mouths to push back our chortling giggles. Luckily, by that time, Dad was focused on his speech and didn't notice we were starting our silliness again. Fortunately, we quickly realized that if we focused on his words without looking at each other, we could keep it together long enough to show respect for his efforts to communicate this very important information.

"I've come to the conclusion", Dad continued, "that we could get rid of the walker, commode, oxygen machine and medical supplies. Those things are for the physical and I am no longer interested in the physical. You can keep the couch and other furniture for you and your mother to use, but I won't be needing any of it". Then he walked a few steps and placed his arms around me. Quietly he asked. "Do you understand what I'm saying, honey? In a few days there will be fireworks". Looking up at him I whispered back, "I understand completely", my heart clenching onto his love. "And I'm so impressed at how you are doing this" I added. "Thank you", he replied with an air of satisfaction as his lips met my forehead. Then he reached out for a hug from his son. Mom began hobbling toward him, her walker clunking across the floor. Her husband turned in her direction and made his way to her. When their walkers touched, they both leaned to each other and their lips came together. He slept very peacefully that night.

By the time the sun rose in the morning the light of the new day brought a new struggle for my father. For mid-December, the weather was amazing; birds singing, clear blue skies, so different from the dreary dark winter days that we were accustomed to. The letting go process thus far had seemed easy enough, at least from my point of view, as he drifted between the physical and spiritual realms the day before, but I soon began to realize that these reminders of how beautiful physical nature can be may have changed his mind. Perhaps the personality of physical reality had strengthened her grip on my dying father during the night as he dreamt of places, events and people who gave meaning to the life that he lived. "I still have some fight left in me", my father disclosed upon awakening in the morning. "I can't give up. I will never give up! How can I ever give up on this world?"

My father was taught since his childhood to never give up, always keep trying, whether it is in relationships, a job, or hopes, dreams and aspirations. "I lived a successful life", he shared. "I wasn't famous and didn't do anything that changed the world on a large scale but I lived the kind of life I wanted. I've been kind to people and I figured out early on that there is something I can learn from everybody. Even when the time came that my supervisors at work were half my age, I recognized that even though they were young, they knew some things that I didn't. And I respected that and I was happy to learn from them and felt proud that they could also learn from me. I had a good life even when there were problems. If I give up, it will mean my life wasn't worth living.". "I understand your dilemma, Dad, but that is not true. There is a world of difference between giving up and letting go. Giving up limits your opportunities because it allows fear to get the best of you, whereas letting go is freeing and expansive. Giving up creates a feeling of self-defeat and feels like a kind of prison. Letting go feels good. When you let go it doesn't mean that you no longer care about anything, it means that you trust God enough to take over. It means that you are satisfied with what you have accomplished, whether in relationships or activities, and all that satisfaction just blends with God's love and is dispersed into the universe to continue on. Letting go gives you the freedom to expand more. Perhaps," I said pausing as my speech wound down, "it's a path to the promised land". My father just nodded and then became quiet. I could tell that he reflected on what I had said. I just let him be.

MIDNIGHT

Chapter Twenty-Two

*"Ah, but a man's reach should exceed his
grasp, or what's a heaven for?"*
~ Robert Browning

As my father's body weakened and he wanted to sit up, I found myself sitting on his bed beside him for long periods of time to prop him up while he silently contemplated his life. Every once in a while he would make a comment or ask a question, although there were not any heavy-duty conversations. I had gotten accustomed to the routine, often entering into my own quiet meditative state while he was in his.

On one such afternoon, the tranquil stillness was rippled by my father's soft voice, "How do I open that door?" he asked, turning his head to make direct eye contact with me while pointing to the dark paneled wall in front of us. I wasn't sure how to respond to his question but luckily I was able to immediately come up with a stalling tactic. "The first thing you need to do is to stand up, Dad", I answered, hoping that by the time he was standing which was a process that I knew would take some time, I would think of what to say next. I slowly helped him to a standing position. Finally up on his feet, his right arm reached out in front of him and his hand was bent up as if in a pushing stance, "That's it?" he asked, sounding surprised. "That was easy." At that point, he seemed to return to his own private world, a world that he was not including me in. I breathed a sigh of relief.

There was no more conversation until the hospice chaplain showed up later in the day. The moment the clergyman walked in the door, dad blurted out that he was having a hard time finding the right "hook-up" and added that he had been very frustrated about it all afternoon. The chaplain wasn't sure how to respond and I, too, was baffled, so hoping for more clarity, I asked my father if it had anything to do with the door he spoke of earlier. He glared at me in disbelief as if it should have been obvious to me what he had been struggling with for the past few hours. "Yes, OF COURSE it does! It has EVERYTHING to do with it!" he answered back. The chaplain and I immediately took turns asking questions. "Did you open the door?" asked the chaplain. "Yes", Dad replied. "Did you go in?" I questioned. "I peeked in", he said. "What did you see?" asked the chaplain. My father said only one word. "Hookups". At that moment, my eyes caught my brothers eyes and we were about to burst out laughing again, not that it was so funny, it was just so unexpected. Even the corners of the chaplain's mouth turned up into a slight smile. But as Bob and I had learned the night before, laughing at this point in time would not be a good idea, even if it were to relieve some of our own stress, and so we both made a special effort not to look at each other. The room grew silent and Dad would say no more as he sat pondering and engulfing himself in his own world once again.

Mom had been sitting at the counter with her Ghanaian companion who spent a good part of her days sitting beside her to ensure that she didn't fall over. My mother was typically in and out of awareness, depending upon when her scheduled medications kicked in, but at that particular moment she was surprisingly alert. When she noticed the lull in conversation, she quickly utilized the opportunity to discuss her concerns and feelings about her own illness with the chaplain. who always made an effort to have some private time with each of us. And so he traded seats with Florence. Mom always enjoyed special attention from all of those who would give it to her but this time proved to be a truly healing moment for her. I was grateful that she was able to express herself and find some comfort.

The chaplain always ended his visits with a prayer. On this day, as we all gathered and held hands, he called out to God, the Lord of our existence:

Dear God,
I pray that you surround this family with your love in this time of physical, emotional and spiritual need.

Help them to cope with the challenges they are facing.
Comfort and encourage them, as well as all those whose lives have been unsettled and disrupted by illness.
I pray for their patience and understanding.
I pray for their strength and wisdom.
I pray for their healing and for inner peace and that Donald will find the right hookups.
Amen.

After he left, my father added to the earlier discussion. "You know those hook-ups I was telling you about? Well, they help me to get from "room to room" he said, while clarifying that he didn't mean the room that I was in, but the "other rooms" that he goes into. "The two houses have to hook up", he said, "and I'm looking for a specific room, one that I haven't been to yet." I understood that my dad was referring to higher vibrational planes. I also understood that he was making preparations to make his final transition. With that, he tilted his head upward toward the heavens with his arms wide open as if embracing an expanded reality. Then in a weakened, exhausted but confident voice, my father called out, "I want to see the light again! I asked to see the light and you showed me the light for a moment, I want to see the light again!" Perhaps my dad is beginning to let go, I thought.

CHAPTER TWENTY-THREE

"We are all the pieces of what we remember. We hold in ourselves the hopes and fears of those who love us. As long as there is love and memory, there is no true loss."
~ Cassandra Clare

WE ALL KNEW that the time was getting closer, even though there was no change in vital signs. Dad remained in his hospital bed most of the time except for when he chose to lie down on the couch instead. Pancreatic cancer is typically a very painful disease, although my father still hadn't complained much of any physical pain. But just the same, the doctor ordered topical morphine for him. It was in the form of a gel that we were instructed to apply to his inner arms and legs because it would be easily absorbed in areas with finer skin and in areas with a lot of veins and arteries closer to the surface.

He was glad that it wasn't necessary to swallow anything because it was getting more difficult for him. Typically when someone is taking medication for pain, it is ideal to "stay ahead of it" as a preventative measure.

As evening rolled around and Dad was bathed and ready to get tucked in for the night, my sister and I donned our latex gloves to protect ourselves from experiencing the effects of the morphine. Then we applied the gel to our father's limbs. "It's cold", he said in a tired voice as I silently wished him comfort for the remainder of the night. No sooner than I had completed my thought, he began screaming, Get it off! Get it off! My entire body is burning! It's rushing through my whole body! Please get it off! As Donna ran for a wet washcloth, I dialed the hospice nurse. "He's apparently having a bad reaction," she informed me," just wash the application area the best you can to prevent more of the drug from absorbing into his system." Bad reactions to medications seemed to run in our family. On many occasions, just about all of us experienced the opposite effect of what the prescription was supposed to help. That's what turned me toward herbal and other holistic remedies.

The next few days were relatively quiet; Dad was awake but didn't say much. At one point he made mention of the baby sitting in the easy chair, still wondering why that kid's mother wasn't with him. He also mentioned a spirit gentleman who often came to sit with him when I was busy elsewhere in the house. This man was to hail a taxi in the event that the time came to do so. "I will need a ride back home" my father told me matter-of-factly. I was reminded of my dream that I shared earlier in which there was man who sat on a bench with my uncle and the baby as if waiting for a bus.

During this time, one of Donna's little dogs became gravely ill and she made the decision to go back home for few days in order to take him to her regular veterinarian who was familiar with her pets. Two weeks previously, she had mentioned that Max wasn't acting like himself, but she didn't elaborate. When she awakened in the morning she realized he had taken a turn for the worse and was deeply concerned. She also hadn't seen her husband in weeks. So she packed up her four furry friends and left for three days.

That weekend we were unaware of the extent of the crisis that Donna was dealing with. Sadly, little Max was diagnosed with a very progressive cancer and was given only days, if not hours, to live. After burying her little friend, my sister returned on Sunday with the remaining three of her beloved pets, only to face what would be the last week of her father's life.

Monday morning brought calm, balmy weather outside but there was an air of restlessness inside the house. Not for Dad, but for the rest of us. He was resting comfortably while the rest of us faced a sort of low-grade, monotone-like anxiety amongst us and our surroundings. It was an atmosphere that was new to us and we feared it was the quiet before the storm.

The chaplain visited that afternoon, as he would continue to do daily for the remainder of the week. Nurses quietly took vital signs in regular intervals, which were still in the normal range. The minutes and hours ticked by slowly and all remained quiet in the house. Few words were spoken by anyone. Since I knew that Dad was relatively stable for the time being, I used the opportunity to get out for an hour and quickly run some errands. It was good to get some fresh air and to enjoy a change of scenery. Luckily, all was well when I returned, or perhaps I could say that nothing was worse, which, in itself, was a blessing.

"I think I'd like a beer" my father spoke out in a weakened voice when Bob entered the house that evening. Dad had slept for most of the day, waking only for a few minutes every few hours. You want a *beer*? My brother questioned, surprised at the request. It had been over a year since a cold beer graced our father's tongue. "Yes, I just want to taste it one last time", he explained. It occurred to me that Dad may have been thinking about this all day as his body rested. But no words were necessary until his son arrived. "I want you to have a beer with me" he said again. "Can you swallow?" Bob asked, trying to be practical. Our father hadn't taken any food for several weeks and fluids had been minimal. The day before, he had drunk what had amounted to a thimbleful of water. And what a difference it made in the dead-flat finish that coated his eyes! The small drops of water instantly filled his tear ducts with moisture, giving our father's dark brown eyes a shiny, glossy finish, framed by the deep boney holes that made up his eye sockets. Perhaps a beer might for a short moment, give us back the dad we remembered before this disease began wasting his body away, I thought. It brought my mind back to the times when as teenagers, he would offer us an occasional beer and eventually other alcoholic beverages under his roof and under his supervision "to give us an education". I learned very quickly that I didn't like beer, wine or other alcohol, and so never took up drinking it as an adult. The buzz I got left me in an uncomfortable feeling of not being in control. Donna learned that she really liked beer but shouldn't drink too much. Bob learned that having a beer with his dad was a bonding experience and as an adult, enjoyed those special times hanging out with him .

"Okay, Dad, let's have a beer." Bob responded after quickly thinking it over. Then he left the room to fulfil the request. He came back with a bottle of Heineken and a shot glass in which to pour a sip for his father. As Bob held up the bottle for a toast, our father's unsteady, shaking hand followed suit raising the shot glass as high as his weak arm could hold it. Then he slowly moved it to his lips before tipping it ever so slightly to allow the liquid to meet his awaiting, opened mouth; the last beer of his life. My brother's last beer with his dad. This cherished moment in time seemed to move in slow motion. As an observer, I could almost feel their thoughts; a sacred and holy moment for my two best men, I thought.

Then tragically, without warning and completely unexpectedly, the whole thing suddenly went sour. "PTEEW!" our father uttered with an exasperated snort as his skeleton face contorted and he made an attempt to spit out the drop of brew that had reached his dry tongue. "That didn't taste like I thought it would", he murmured, partly in shock and partly sobbing. Bob's expectations of this anticipated special moment was also destroyed. It was heartbreaking to witness their disappointment. Most likely, between the medications and his body beginning to shut down, our father's chemistry had changed, making the Heineken unpalatable. The three of us sat silently reflecting on this defeat, a loss none of us had foreseen. It was just a week or so before, I recalled, when my father stoically announced that there would be no more physical. Apparently, drinking a beer was included in that. With that realization, I caught a glance of the big red, overstuffed, clown-like, cartoon slippers positioned neatly beside the bed patiently awaiting my father's feet. I was well aware that those silly slippers would be doing no more walking and no more dancing.

Chapter Twenty-Four

"Knock-knock-knockin' on heaven's door."
~ Bob Dylan

As the week wore on, Dad was sleeping more and was speaking less but appeared increasingly relaxed when he was awake. He seemed comforted by the individual attention that he received from his wife, daughters and son. Mom would sit with her husband every morning for at least two hours, holding his hand, adjusting his pillow and blankets and silently communicating as longtime couples do. This was the man who had loved her for over fifty-four years. Yes, they had their ups and downs, but had remained committed and devoted to each other for the long haul. He had spent the last four years putting his own life activities aside to tend to his wife's every need throughout her painful and difficult illness, and now she sat beside him in a reversed position, doing her best to cater to his needs despite her pain and own limitations. Even though she was still as disabled as before, by contrast, she was now the stronger of the two.

My siblings and I allowed each other the private time that we needed with our dying father as he drifted in and out of consciousness. Other times during those long final days, we all gathered together on the couch quietly talking and laughing while reminiscing about happy times as he lay in his hospital bed in front of us with his eyes closed. We were cognizant of his need for space and made efforts not to hover. Although he appeared to be asleep, perhaps he was listening from afar, from an outside perspective as he had done the previous month when the extended family visited at the dining table. He wanted us to celebrate, be happy and go on with our lives.

The next morning brought a change in heart rate and breathing patterns. Mom, even in her highly medicated state, instinctively knew that her husband's journey would soon come to an end. She was the first to go to his side even before hearing the update in his condition. When she reached for his hand, I overheard him tell her he loved her and so I left them to cherish their moment alone together. Dad was sound asleep by the time Florence called Mom to breakfast.

It wasn't long before Donna secured a spot on the couch near her father. Whether or not words were spoken, I do not know, but the grace, beauty and love surrounding them felt holy and sacred as I glanced in their direction from the other room.

Bob took advantage of the moment as well, creating an envelope of space for himself and his dad. To stay close and do nothing was all that was needed.

When I entered the room I knelt on the floor by my father's bed. Although his eyes were wide open, he seemed to be staring into an empty, blank space. "Can you see?" I questioned. He did not move, did not even blink. Then after a moment, he turned his head in the direction of my voice, slowly and deliberately shook his head from side to side and then quietly responded "not with physical eyes." Little did I know that those would be the last words I heard from my father's mouth.

Chapter Twenty-Five

"Death is not extinguishing the light; it is only putting out the lamp because the dawn has come."
~ Rabindranath Tagore

Florence, who normally went home at 6pm, had made the decision to stay the night since she anticipated that we might need her help. As the evening hours ticked nearer, Mom was becoming increasingly anxious and spent most of her time in her clunking walker moving back and forth from room to room. Generally, at dinnertime, on all nights but this one, she would sit for hours still propped up at the counter from breakfast, eating her evening meal and watching the small television that sat in the corner part of the counter-top. After finally convincing her to sit, Florence did her best to distract her from her restlessness with the collection of mail order catalogues that were piled up neatly beside the TV. Perhaps this would transport my mother's restless mind to another place in time when unusual and useful gadgets and gizmos offered hope for making even the most difficult daily tasks a bit easier. After all, who wouldn't need a contraption to make square hard boiled eggs? But it was the organizers that had always gotten my mother's attention. She had always been a pack-rat but at least she was neat and tidy about it. If only there were a gadget that would keep the emotions surrounding the loss of a lifelong partner neatly packed up and organized so they could be worked through and understood systematically. How nice it would be if that gadget could guarantee that healing would take place evenly and consistently throughout the days and weeks ahead. The random emotional ups and downs of this journey had been exhausting for everyone.

As secretions built up in Dad's airway and throat due to his being too weak to clear them out, a soft rattling sound reverberated through the room with every breath he took. The accumulation of mucus and fluids at this stage of the dying process often sounds uncomfortable for patients and can be quite distressing for loved ones, however, it is generally accepted by the medical community that there is no impact of the "death rattle" on a patient's comfort.

As Dad's breathing became more labored, the level of anxiety in the air grew stronger. We all knew that death was imminent and that the final waiting game had begun. We were already physically and emotionally exhausted from the long ride thus far, as well as from what might lie ahead in the coming weeks and months. We had hoped to get mom settled into bed, so that we too, might be able to relax somewhat before our lives dramatically changed. But always a woman who did things her own way, she would have no part of it. She insisted on staying awake and walking the course from her husband's hospital bed in the living room and then down the long hallway to what had become her own bedroom, and then repeating the trek over and over again. The sound of her walker clunking across the floor was nerve-racking as it played like a drum on the downbeat of the song of death coming from our father's throat.

Florence was already fast asleep on Dad's black leather recliner with a crocheted blanket draped over her tired body. Donna had settled into her usual spot on the winterized porch, snug in her sleeping bag on the daybed, her three dogs snoring loudly on the floor beside her. Bob crashed on the guest room bed without even going under the covers.

I was left alone by my siblings to be on "Mom duty". Finally, she could walk no more and so I convinced her to go to bed at last. No sooner than I had tucked her in, I could hear the hum of snoring escaping from her wind instrument, too.

I was very tired. All was finally quiet in the house with the exception of my father's loud and labored breathing. But despite the ominous sound, he looked peaceful and comfortable. "I think I will pull up a stool and sit by him" I thought, "and breathe with him. Everyone is asleep so no one will know if I'm hovering", I selfishly decided. So I pulled over a small fold-up stool, wrapped myself in a blanket and matched my breathing with his. After a few breaths, I skipped half a breath so that when he breathed in, I would breathe out, when he breathed out, I would breathe in. It was difficult this time because now his breaths were very irregular. I counted up to sixty seconds between some of his gasps and gulps of air. I was beginning to feel cold sitting on that uncomfortable stool even with the blanket wrapped around me. And I was so incredibly tired. Maybe I should lie down on the couch with more blankets to keep me warm, I thought. I could continue to breathe with Dad, as I have to breathe anyway, I reasoned. And so, it was settled. I rose from the stool and pushed it away to remove any evidence of my hovering, and then sandwiched myself on the couch between several warm, cozy blankets. It was so good to finally lie down! From this position, I consciously resumed the infinity breathing that I had started with my father, while forcing my tired and heavy eyes to remain open. Every once in a while I would catch my lids drooping and so forcefully raised my eyebrows to keep my drowsy lids in an open position. Maybe I can close them just for a moment, I thought. I could still breathe with my father with my eyes shut. And so, it was settled, and that is just what I did. Still awake but with my eyes closed, I concentrated on my breathing, matching breaths with my fathers. My eyeballs were happy to relax. Then, without me knowing, I must have dozed off because I suddenly felt myself waking up. It was for only a moment that I snoozed, but enough for me to become disoriented. The house was especially quiet. Something was different, but in my mind-fogged state,

I couldn't quite put my finger on what it was. I looked over at my father, "He is resting comfortably" I thought. From my vantage point, I could see his chest rise and fall. "What is different?" I asked myself again. My eyes quickly swept the room as if looking for a clue. Florence was still asleep in the recliner chair. Then I remembered! Florence spent the night because my father's death was imminent! I could no longer hear his gasps! I burst out from the warm blankets that covered me and placed my hand on his chest. It was only then that I realized there was no heartbeat or breathing as he laid there motionless. Apparently, I had only imagined my father's chest rising just a moment ago, because that is what my brain was used to seeing, but this time, it was only an illusion.

A serene and tranquil stillness shrouded the room. Except for Florence still asleep nearby, I found myself breathing alone. Aware of my breaths, I took a moment to embrace the quietude, and then chuckled to myself at how my father left this world exactly in the manner that he had hoped. His family was nearby but not hovering over him. Not even me.

Chapter Twenty-Six

"Seeing death as the end of life is like seeing the horizon as the end of the ocean."
~ David Searls

Sensing it was time that I step away from the holy area of the house where my dad's spirit was brought home, I made my way down the hall to where Bob was sleeping. "Bob, wake up," I whispered, to break the news. "Dad is gone" "What?!?" he moaned groggily and stunned, "I just got to bed, it hasn't even been a half hour!" as if not understanding how the angel of death could come for his father so quickly.

Upon hearing the movement in the house, Donna was already awake when my brother and I entered to verify her suspicions. "I'd like to see him before waking mom", she said quietly. "Me too", Bob agreed somberly. As Dad's three children gathered around his lifeless body, Florence still slept like a rock. Even though we all occupied the same spot in the room, individually, our minds drifted to our own private space to react and reflect on the site in front of us.

We all agreed to awaken Florence next, to help us with mom. I had dreaded this moment; informing my mother that her husband had left this world, but as a family, we combined our strength and slowly marched to her room. Like Donna, she was already awake. "Can I see him?" she asked, as if we would say no. It was the first time in my life that I had ever heard my mother ask permission to do what she wanted to do. Upon reaching his body, we left her alone with him.

In the meantime, Donna and I were discussing the next steps with Florence while Bob set out on a mission rummaging through the cabinet that was situated between the kitchen and the dining room. As I peeked into the living room to check on my mother, I could see that she was no longer leaning over her husband from her wheelchair, but instead was sitting back with her hands folded neatly in her lap and displaying a blank look on her face, appearing as if she were on the other side of the bridge that connected the fifty-four years she once knew.

As Donna, Florence and I returned to the couch, Bob entered the room handing out shot glasses. "Dad would want a toast" he said, determined to make this salute better than the last.

Conclusion

"I am left standing here holding the blessing and I give thanks to God."
~ Eckhart Tolle

FLORENCE INSTRUCTED ME to bring a wash basin filled with warm water, soap, a wash cloth, and towels along with clean clothes. I had never prepared a deceased body before nor had I ever even thought about doing it myself, so I was glad to have her there to lead in this ritual. Washing and dressing the body is, in all cultures, an act of intimacy and a sign of respect for the dead and considered to be the ultimate kindness. Since I was the one who was most involved in my father's physical care, I spontaneously fell into the role of taking part in this reverent act while my siblings and mother sat solemnly on the couch nearby as witnesses to the holy procedure.

When she was ready to begin, Florence softly placed her forefinger on my father's lids and gently closed his eyes. Then, taking the warm, damp washcloth in her hand she tenderly wiped his face and then slowly progressed to his neck as I patted him dry with a towel after her. When it was time to remove his shirt, she motioned for me to cover his bare chest with the thick soft bath towel while she bathed his arms. Her continued respect for my father's modesty and "comfort" was heartwarming. She continued on with the process, gently moving and turning his body as necessary and then re-dressing each area of the body with fresh clothing before moving on.

When the ceremonial rite of passage was complete, the human shell that had housed my father's soul for seventy-six years laid still, arms positioned at its side, the circle of this life complete and standing by to return back to dust.

I was reminded again of the things my father's hands built over the years, constructing and re-constructing as needs changed and time passed; and how his open and kind heart had embraced us all throughout his lifetime here on earth. I thought about how grateful I was to have had the opportunity to witness my father constructing his holy internal temple during his dying time for the continuation of his soul's journey. And with that, I was left standing there holding the blessing and giving the glory and thanks to God.

Afterward

Over a decade has passed since my dad made his journey home and since I began this book project. A lot has happened in the meantime. First and foremost, when I think of my father's long battle, even through all of the pain, suffering and heartaches, we, as a family, changed in positive ways. We had always been a family in which each of us had prided ourselves on our independence. But during this struggle, we had all moved from being independent to being inter-dependent, and this, I think, is what family is all about. My siblings and I became closer and understand each other a lot better than before the ordeal and for this, we are blessed.

We had chosen a floral-shaped, bio-degradable container for an ocean burial. Because Donna and her husband owned a boat, we didn't have to worry about finding someone who was willing and able to help us with this phase of our healing journey--delivering the cremains into Long Island Sound.

The August day we had scheduled brought us clear blue skies and an abundance of warm sunshine. Mom's live-in companion had taken the weekend off so the agency sent a substitute. This routine had become customary at least once a month since she came on with our family eight months before. The young lady they sent wasn't one we had met before, as she was new to the agency. Bob was feeling bad for her because of the fact that her first day on the job she would be subjected to attending a burial, and so he offered her the option of staying home alone in an unfamiliar house or coming along with us. She liked the idea of going out on the boat and decided to join us.

Mom had purchased five cremation memory lockets for me, Donna, Sharon, Saida and herself to fill with her husband's ashes that were meant to be worn on a chain as a necklace to keep a loved one's memory near to the heart. Bob had been gifted with a sterling silver egg-shaped container to be used for the same purpose. My family had nominated me to pour the box of our father's, grandfather's and husband's burned and disintegrated body into the bio-degradable container. I then carefully filled the tiny filigreed heart and cylinder-shaped charms using a miniature spoon. After my creepy task was complete, Mom slowly removed the wedding ring that had encircled her finger for fifty-four years and then gently buried it in the pile of ash. "Are you sure you want to do that, Mom?" I asked. "I gave it deep thought" she said, "and it's what I want to do". I don't ever remember seeing my mother so certain and so calm and composed than she had been at that moment.

Bob, who was good at assembling things, tenderly secured the decorative, floral cover to the base of the container and then put the whole thing back into the sturdy box that it came in. When we were ready to head down to the place where the boat was docked, he protectively carried it to his car, making sure to keep its contents level.

I wasn't sure how solid a plan we had once we reached the boat, but it turned out that we would just go with the flow. And so, Donna and her husband, Bob and his wife, Aunt Ann, the caregiver, my mother and I piled onto the vessel and sat in seats that Donna assigned to us to keep the weight in balance to prevent the boat from tipping over. We set out into the sound traveling in a direction that would take us to a spot that we calculated was directly in line with our childhood home which was located about a mile from the shore. It wasn't long before the boat came to a halt and our captain lowered the anchor. The plan was to place the container in the water and watch it float until it slowly melted away. We were told by the funeral director who sold it to us that this could take five to seven minutes. Our cameras were ready to capture the somber moments.

I have never been a fan of boats due to a longtime fear of deep water. I'm not sure how it ended up being me who was expected to carry the floral, bio-degradable container onto the stern and release the funerary parcel into the softly bobbing waves.

In total fear of falling overboard, I moved with intense caution, slowly inching my way onto the stern. Its gate was wide open so that I could stand ever-so-close to the edge and have a better chance at tossing the heavy box filled with remnants of my father's smile, his dark brown eyes, and warm bear hugs out far enough as to not get caught in the boats propeller. Had I been physically stronger, I probably would not have tilted the weighty container as much as I had, causing its contents to shift all the way to one side as I heaved it as far from the boat as my inadequate arms could get it. The instant it hit the water, it took a rapid nosedive downward and was swallowed up by the unpredictable, deep, blue ocean water. It was just a moment in time and he was gone.

My mother had spent the first four years of living without her husband being helped by several live-in caregivers. Independent and stubborn, she was typically not one to let people do things for her, however she had no choice but to adjust to this change after reluctantly realizing that her abilities and mobility were limited enough that she could not care for herself. Soon after Dad passed, in the interim few weeks before the live-in help arrived, my siblings and I still continued to stay with her around the clock. Just before the New Year, Mom was rushed to the hospital by ambulance after nearly bleeding out from a stomach ulcer caused by the aspirins prescribed for her heart, leaving her teetering on the brink of death. This was a wake-up call for her, reminding her that even though she followed the prescribed treatment plan, unexpected things could happen, and therefore, it was good to have someone with her. She was too stubborn to leave this world without a fight, and so, with the new life change looming in front of her, she resigned to it, knowing that this time, she must carefully pick her battles.

The first live-in companion was a lovely woman from Lithuania with a no-nonsense personality who was determined to wean Mom (with the approval of her physician) off the prescribed opioid that left her with unwanted side effects and that was no longer helping her condition. The caregiver's success at this task was instrumental in allowing our mother to enjoy a greatly improved quality of life, so much so that she was able to resume some of the activities that she previously loved, such as her art, going to events around town, and visiting with friends, despite still suffering from severe chronic pain and still wobbly on her feet. However, even with those challenges, it was truly a gift that she had some normalcy in her life again, especially during the grieving period after the loss of her longtime husband.

A year and half after getting somewhat comfortable in her new life, our mothers caregiver faced her own family issues and needed to return to her native country. Mom was never one to easily accept change. This was a huge blow to us all. We had no choice but to call the agency and begin interviewing more prospective caregivers. Luckily, we were quickly able to come to an agreement and make a decision about which girl to hire with our mother's feedback, however, it was no sooner had she moved in when mom suffered a stroke. This resulted in her needing a lot more help than before. To the relief of my siblings and I, the new companion was trained by the hospital staff in how to best care for our mother.

Maybe I shouldn't say that my mother was a control freak, but definitely, the fact remains that a control freak she was. She always wore the pants in the house, as they say, and Dad permitted and tolerated it. "Happy wife - Happy life" he reasoned. He, too, carefully picked his battles.

Slowly but surely since the start of her illness, Mom had been losing control of many aspects of her life, especially after suffering the stroke. Unfortunately, her control-freakishness was to be her biggest challenge to overcome. The new girl, who was also headstrong and a perfectionist like my mother, displayed strengths that were focused on the physical aspects of caregiving. She kept a rigid schedule and always completed everything on her daily list. But Mom was not used to obeying anybody. They often butted heads and their personal relationship was very strained. But as time went on, bit by bit, mom's stubbornness mellowed considerably as dementia began to set in. She eventually contended with two more caregivers, the last, being her favorite; a very smart, happy-go-lucky woman, also from Eastern Europe like the others. Their personalities worked well together and they became close. But, in 2010, the time had come for the need for Mom to adjust to another major change.

After long discussions between me and my siblings, we agreed to give our mother the option to either move into a nursing home facility or she could live in my home with me. It would be her choice. She chose me.

Quite frankly, when she made the big move, aside from the truck load of her stuff that my brother dumped at my house that I would need to find a place for, I was a bit worried about how she would deal with more changes and how her response to those changes might affect me. Fortunately, by this stage of our lives, we had gradually resolved much of the mother-daughter challenges that had plagued us in earlier years. However, the mother who stood before me was not the healthy mother I had once known. This mother was in constant, debilitating pain almost every minute of every day since 2002, and I didn't think I could help her in that area. Interestingly, once she had settled into my house I found that she rarely complained about pain even though I knew she suffered greatly. She didn't complain about anything for that matter, and put forth every effort to put on a happy face. As independent and stubborn as I had always known her personality to be, in this case her stubbornness came in handy! She would be damned if she would let #10 pain ruin her day!

Early on, I had started the practice of providing my mother with daily hugs. Even though she had never been one to express affection in that way, I had read that our bodies and brains actually need daily hugs to keep us healthy. Hugs are known to increase the levels of the "love hormone" oxytocin, which can help to reduce stress, improve heart health and even boost the immune system. So the decision to initiate hugs was a no brainer for me, I knew it would be beneficial for both of us if she would agree to it and most certainly we were both hug deprived. Every night before I tucked her in, we would pause for ten minutes and sit at the edge of her bed in a genuine embrace, sometimes talking, sometimes not, when we would just let our minds wander. On one mind-wandering evening, she broke the silence. "Once when Grammy was up from Florida, this was when Donna was a toddler, she explained, "I dressed her up in a little yellow dress. She looked so cute in it and I said to Donna, "You look so beautiful today!" And she did, especially with her gorgeous, curly blond hair. Grammy snapped at me "You should NEVER compliment a child, especially on how they look!" I was a new mother with no experience in raising a child. We were taught to honor, respect and obey Mother, so that's what I did". Hmmmm, I thought. That explains a lot.

During our first year living together, my mother resigned to the fact that she was no longer able to tap dance or clog, ride horses, or participate in other physical activities as she did in her past, so instead she enjoyed reading, watching TV, eating, sleeping and all things related to the mirror, such as teeth brushing and eyebrow plucking. At first, I made every attempt to get her out to town concerts and other events, which was also good for me and my own sanity, but even with the help of the stair glide that had been installed in my house, and along with the wheel chair and walker, it was a long process to get her out as her mobility continued to decline.

By year two after my mother's condition held me captive in my house for twenty-three hours each day, allowing me only a quick trip to the gym or the store while she napped, I was ready for a break. As luck would have it, I learned that my mother qualified to receive benefits from a state program that offered services aimed at allowing the elderly and disabled a way to stay at home and receive the special care that they needed, while being less costly than being placed in a nursing home. It also provided respite for caretakers; all for just a minimal, sliding scale fee. I thought that this program would help us both considerably. Mom was matched up with a wonderful companion named Cheryl, who stayed with her on Mondays to give me some respite time away from my caregiving duties. Cheryl was patient, happy and cheerful and did wonders for my mother's social needs.

Mom had always been a social butterfly and had been blessed with a whole repertoire of devoted friends to support her diverse interests and hobbies throughout her life. One thing that stood out about her is that she was always very organized, and in my opinion, to the point of OCD. She was good at categorizing not only things but people, too, and amusingly, she went by a different name for every group of friends or family that she associated with. Since she liked a variety of things, each specific interest corresponded to one of her names. This may have confused a lot of people but to my mother, it made sense. And similar to me, she marched to a different drummer. I remember her always being busy, constantly moving from one thing to another. As she shifted from activity to activity, her name would change. If you were associated with any of my father's side of the family, you probably knew her as Tess. If you worked with her, she was Theresa, if you were involved with anything artsy, you called her Terry. If you met her in her belly dancing phase, she was Terka and if you knew her through her own side of the family, you would call her Grace (the name she despised since she was a little girl, the name she often took great effort not to respond to when addressed by it), And then of course there was Mom, Mother, Gramma, and then later, to our shock and disbelief, the self-proclaimed "Gramma Grace" when her great - grandkids came into the picture! We have no idea how that happened but when she came to live me, she decided to be called Grace!

By year three, after a number of falls, hospital visits and small surgeries, advancing dementia, and continued stroke and nerve related problems, she began to slow down a lot. She discontinued reading due to being unable to comprehend the meanings of the sentences which resulted in her being glued to the TV more. Although she couldn't follow what was happening in the programs, she enjoyed the pictures. Every time a program ended, she would turn to me shrugging her shoulders with a dumbfounded look on her face and say "I don't get it". "Don't worry," I always assured her, "it was a dumb show anyway". By this time, she needed much more of my help with daily living activities. We reached a point when we didn't converse much; I talked to her but she didn't respond a great deal because the stroke left her unable to get the correct words out and it frustrated her enough that she gave up trying. I suppose that her stubborn will was relaxing a bit too.

Throughout year four in my home, her life had become completely different than it had ever been before, but I think the most significant change, aside from the physical deterioration, was that every new person that she had met since she came to stay in my home, had called her Grace. As she became more comfortable living in her "Grace" name, she sometimes reverted back to when she was a young girl. There were times when she would respond to me as if I were her mother or one of her sisters. I began to learn a little bit about her childhood, not because she talked to me about it, except for a few snippets from our hugging sessions, but because of her responses to what she imagined was going on. I began to form a sort of emotional profile of her that was expressed through her feelings and reactions. Although I may not have always realized it in every instance, I was playing the role of her mother or of one of her sisters in either her imagined or déjà vu circumstances. On this stage, aside from a few occasions when we would get into a power struggle about bedtime or some other daily event, I apparently didn't normally respond the way she expected me to, had I actually been one of those other people who she thought I was. Sometimes when she was able to get some words out of her mouth, she would say, "Mother, why are you being so kind to me?" Gradually, my mother began to get even more relaxed in her Grace skin, less resistant than I previously had known her to be. On some occasions, she even asked for help when she needed it if I was not already aware. Although I'm not sure who she thought I was in many of these circumstances, she knew that she was Grace. I believe that somehow, by the grace of God, we became staged in a way that allowed her to work through unresolved struggles from her past. And interestingly, as a witness to this, it helped me to understand not only some specific circumstances of her past, but the library of feelings that we both carried that led up to some of the mother-daughter challenges that we had faced earlier on in my life. In reference to the circle of life, I realized that my mother, Grace McLaughlin Kish, (Jan 30,1933 - June 21, 2014) eventually came full circle in her lifetime, beginning where it ended and ending where it began, and I truly feel blessed to have been a part of it. Amazing Grace.

After college, Saida graduated with a master's degree in accounting and became a CPA. At that time, she was employed as an auditor with clients in many locations and had often worked late into the dark evening hours. It was common for her to call me on speaker phone during her drive back home to check in and tell me about her day. On one such evening, I answered to her terrified voice, "Mom! I'm walking through the parking lot at work and there is someone sitting in the front seat of my car!" She sounded totally panicked. "Turn around and run back to the building", I ordered in horror. I was left helpless to do anything and I didn't even know where she was working that day, "and call the police!" I added, "and then call me right back".

I waited for what seemed like forever; petrified in the spot I had been standing with the phone in my hand and my finger ready to press the "answer" button. And then finally, even though in reality it had only been a minute or two later, her call came in. The girl on the other end was laughing. "When I started to turn around, I saw from a different view and the person in my car was gone. Then I looked carefully again from another angle", she excitedly explained, "and I saw him again. It was just Grandpa waiting for me!

Since that day until now, she often senses her grandfather around her, "He's usually sitting in my office at work just waiting for me to arrive or to go home—I'm used to it now" she told me one day. "That's comforting", I said with my heart wearing a smile.

I recently visited Rashid, who has put down roots in California with his fiancé. Over the years he has steadily climbed the ladder in his profession and reached long-time goals by accepting new positions in various retail corporations around the country. He finally settled himself with Pacific Sunwear (also known as PacSun). "I know that Grandpa hangs around me and has been helping me", he casually informed me during my visit. "Did you know that a few months ago PacSun and Eddie Bauer merged to form a new operating company?" I was amazed. Now that's a full circle I never would have expected!

As we begin to grasp the enormity of our creation and existence, we can surely understand that we don't die and that life is continuous. Heaven is not a place, it is a *system* – a system of subtle energies that are constantly stirring about and creating new effects that help shape and transform our daily lives. The earth plane is not separate from this system; it is merely the physical component of it. The system that sustains us in life is the same system that sustains us in death.

ABOUT THE AUTHOR

Karin Nemri has been sensitive to the inner light of others since she was young girl visiting isolated seniors in a nursing home that was located in her neighborhood. Her gift of being able to connect to the spirit of others became even more pronounced after her near death experience as a teen, which led her on a lifetime healing path to help not only other people but herself, too.

Karin is a Certified Spiritual Counselor, Aiijii Healer and lecturer as well as a certified Domestic Violence Counselor with an Associate's Degree in Human Services. She has volunteered hundreds of hours of her time with hospice in various nursing homes since 1996. From 2000-2004 she was the chairperson of the Connecticut Affiliate of The Twilight Brigade: *Compassion in Action*, where she organized and co-facilitated training for hospice volunteers. Karin also served on the steering committee of the Hospice - Veterans Partnership of Connecticut and was active in The Connecticut Coalition to Improve End-of-Life Care. After the tragedy of 9-11, she was trained for the Connecticut Emergency Crisis Response Team/Spiritual Division. Karin was also a member of the Connecticut Holistic Health Organization and served as the Ombudsman for a local nursing home. She has been a board member of the Academy for Spiritual and Consciousness Studies, Inc. since 2006.

Karin is also an accomplished portrait artist. Her work is known for its vibrant colors and her ability to capture the soul of her subjects. She lives in Bloomfield, Connecticut and is the proud grandmother of four grandchildren. "Dancing in the Moonlight: *Embracing the Sacred in the Dying Time*" is her first book. You can contact her at Karin.Nemri@gmail.com

www.ingramcontent.com/pod-product-compliance
Lightning Source LLC
Chambersburg PA
CBHW022101160426
43198CB00008B/311